What people are saying about
Which Button Do You Push to Get God to Come Out?

"A rollicking spiritual journey that is fun, insightful and helpful to women of all ages."

Silvana Clark, speaker, author of twelve books and partner in Soles4Souls Ministry

"I love this devo! Using (LOL) laugh out loud personal experiences, author Jo Russell skillfully weaves Scripture into the craziness of real life and encourages the reader to apply biblical principles to her own harried everyday life. An uplifting and smile-provoking read!"

Debora M. Coty, award-winning author of *Too Blessed to Be Stressed* and *Mom NEEDS Chocolate*

"Want to resign from multitasking through the demands of motherhood, work, and relationships? Jo's stories give hope that God always loves, laughs with us, and provides! Thoughtful questions at the end of each story allow you to ponder how He is working in your life. A delightful journey for all women, including singles!"

Donna Goodrich, author of twenty-two books, 700 published manuscripts, many in Christian publications

"Have you ever thought life would take you down and hold you there forever? Throw out those black thoughts! Each story is a gem, a treasure every one of us needs to cuddle up with every day."

Penny Porter, frequent speaker and author of seven books, contributor to more than ten books and fourteen *Chicken Soup for the Soul* anthologies

Which Button Do You Push to Get *God* to Come Out?

A Humorous Devotional for Women

Enjoy the journey! Jo Russell

By Jo Russell

IPG

Intermedia Publishing Group

Which Button Do You Push to Get God to Come Out?

Published by:
Intermedia Publishing Group, Inc.
P.O. Box 2825
Peoria, Arizona 85380
www.intermediapub.com

ISBN 978-1-935906-61-2

Printed in the United States of America.

Dedication

To my daughters-in-law, Jessica and Maria.
May this help in all the days of your journey
as God's special spiritual women.

Contents

Acknowledgements

With God, all things are possible. With him and this team, great things happened!

My need for humor and a connection with God became a powerful journey with strong ideas developed through these people's vision and knowledge.

Much thanks to my longtime friend, Mysterious Myrtle, who would not want to be named for "putting in commas."

It was always much more than that, as Myrtle, with her love of God and continual commitment to studying the Bible, was the balancing force in these devotionals to know whether the verse and the story belonged together. After one two-and-a-half hour hunt for a verse to match a story, she announced, "Jo, you have to start with the verse. You already have the stories." From then on, I did.

I appreciate her logical-sequential side. It helped me to stop cliff-diving, bird-walking, and beating around the bush.

Of all the meaningful work Myrtle has done since retiring, the most valuable has been fine-tuning me through this book. God is honored with her service and mine.

Well done, God's good and faithful servant, M.M.

Thanks also to Rick at Complete Office Repair, who was the collision specialist every time the computer crashed and when "how to" was above my head. The technological Grand Tetons became sand dunes in his capable hands.

Many thanks to all those who shared their stories. In the case of Grand Mal Embarrassment, I changed many of their names. All the names in the conclusion are correct.

No one ever tires of enough genuine encouragement, and I credit Terry Whalin of Intermedia Publishing with mentoring me as a professional and growing my skills as a writer.

Introduction

This book is not for every woman, but for those who don't have enough joy, laughter, faith and encouragement. Juggling and struggling with the "Superwoman" role has become more colorful and complex over the decades.

Picture this in the want ads:

"Competent woman needed desperately to work full-time as well as to care for nearly perfect children, clean lollipops off the rug when needed, do more loads of wash in a week than the Sudz Bucket Laundry, balance the budget and create fantastic vacations for $$.$$, cook like a chef, create meals for company without eggs and without notice, make time for each member of the family, keep an organized home, find everything that was lost somewhere in the house, delegate chores fairly and age-appropriately to each sibling, get eight hours of sleep (optional), work out regularly (optional), go to school to better one's self and career (also optional), as well as model and teach spiritual principles to family."

Whatever happened to milk-and-cookies and after school moms in aprons? In a few more decades, a child may wonder, "What's an apron?"

At last, here is a book that wraps its words around you with comfort and great love from God. I have been where you are and can giggle about it!

Through this journey, you will know that without God, you can do nothing, but with him you can do anything!

Jo Russell

Books of the Bible

Old Testament:

Genesis
Exodus
Leviticus
Numbers
Deuteronomy
Joshua
Judges
Ruth
1 Samuel
2 Samuel
1 Kings
2 Kings
1 Chronicles
2 Chronicles
Ezra
Nehemiah
Esther
Job
Psalms
Proverbs
Ecclesiastes
Song of Solomon
Isaiah
Jeremiah
Lamentations
Ezekiel
Daniel
Hosea
Joel
Amos
Obadiah
Jonah
Micah
Nahum
Habakkuk
Zephaniah
Haggai
Zechariah
Malachi

New Testament:

Matthew
Mark
Luke
John
Acts
Romans
1 Corinthians
2 Corinthians
Galatians
Ephesians
Philippians
Colossians
1 Thessalonians
2 Thessalonians
1 Timothy
2 Timothy
Titus
Philemon
Hebrews
James
1 Peter
2 Peter
1 John
2 John
3 John
Jude
Revelation

Week 1

Which Button Do You Push to Get God to Come Out?

Day 1

Which Button Do You Push to Get God to Come Out?

> *Jesus answered, "I am the way, and the truth and the life. No one comes to the Father except through me. If you really knew me, you would know my Father as well. From now on, you do know him and have seen him."* John 14:6-7

The rural high school student seated at the computer card catalog looked puzzled and exasperated. All lunch period, the pretty, dark-haired sophomore had been there in front of the screen. Other students came and went around her.

Noticing this, Linda, the librarian, approached the girl. She wondered what the student was researching. Why didn't the girl look around the library for the listing she had on the computer screen?

"Another English class research project?" Linda wondered. "Probably."

The student seemed stuck. Linda moved closer and asked her, "May I help you?"

"I'm trying to find this book." The student pointed to the screen.

"Yes," the librarian replied, "and the book you want is here in the library. No one has it checked out."

Still the teen sat in the chair scanning the screen, the keyboard, the hard drive, looking for anything that would give her a clue as to what to do next.

"Do you need more help?" Linda asked.

"Yes," the student said. "I really need this book! Which button do you push to get the book to come out?"

Even without looking for a button, we can find the way, the truth and the life. The button to push that brings God is the Bible. He speaks to us through it and gives us directions for a better life. Tried it your own way? I did. Try it God's way. Let him surprise you. His answers aren't even in the A-Z alphabet!

Thinking you're going to hit a wall? God moves it!

Rough times and smoother ones are part of the journey. Why not let him guide you every day and laugh at his surprises with me?

Further study: Psalm 19:7-8

Day 2

Can An Almond Be Your Source of Joy?

Jesus said, "If you obey my commandments, you will remain in my love, just as I have obeyed my Father's commands and remain in his love. I have told you this so that my joy will be in you and your joy may be complete." John 15:10-11

Something fell off the kitchen counter in the middle of the night and bounced.

Home alone, I listened in the darkness, then heard a furious clack, bang, and crash!

The police had posted a notice on the doors of our neighborhood that summer. What did it say? Lock your doors and windows! A burglar hit seven homes in the neighborhood, mostly by just walking in. On this hot night, I'd passed out with exhaustion after work and fallen asleep in my clothes.

My heart thumped and I felt icy as my life flashed in front of my eyes. I clasped my hand around heavy metal. It wasn't a Smith and Wesson, but a fitness pack full of drinks, work out clothes, bras, and underwear that could pack a wallop. I sat up and listened for footsteps. None.

Tiptoeing out of bed, I took my defensive stance with the gym bag. More clack, clack, bang! No footsteps. I flattened myself against the walls close to the kitchen, scanned the room and the next, and another, then returned to the kitchen where the noise continued. I flipped on the light and backed away quickly to avoid a bullet. Nothing! Where was the large, clumsy intruder who had entered the house with such a clatter?

An almond shot by my feet. Then a grey streak zig-zagged across the room chasing it until the nut bounced off the baseboards.

Tigger! I stepped forward. Something brown and hard pushed into my bare feet. I was afraid to look. What is a cat litter box for anyway? I lifted my toes off the mound. But it was only a Brazil nut Tigger had propelled across the room.

"Tigger," I growled irritably, and scooped up the energized feline. She purred.

I am taking life's lessons from a cat. She can be perfectly happy just playing with nuts! Almonds, that is.

What did I learn from this? The pure joy of simple experiences. Being loved and held in God's hands every day does bring joy!

For years, my life was more work and no play. Every day, I drove to work through red mesa country that looked like *Arizona Highways Magazine,* but didn't notice. I had missed the moment. Thoughts, plans and worries about the past and the future kept me in a numb state.

Tigger taught me that now is the time to wake up to the joy of today and a thankful heart for each moment in time. God gives us the present. It's a panorama of beauty and experiences like a gift. Tigger had the right idea. Enjoy life now—right down to the last almond!

Where do you find joy today?

Further study: Psalm 84:11; Isaiah 55:9-12

Day 3

Hold the Cranberry Juice, Please!

Show me your ways, O Lord, teach me your paths; guide me in your truth and teach me, for you are God my Savior, and my hope is in you all day long.

Psalm 25:4-5

While the doorbell rang again and again with one child at the door, two young girls were on their knees watching the fresh bread we made bake in the oven. Another boy was making waffles at the dining room table. Everyone in this large family was at my house to learn something.

While his older brother lifted out a light, fluffy waffle he just made, eight-year-old Caleb started to dump the rest of his cranberry juice on a seven-foot ficus tree. Maybe he wanted to share the sweet drink with a plant. More likely, the potted plant was closer than the trash can in the next room.

"Wait!" I cried, "Benjamin Ficus doesn't like cranberry juice!"

"What about this one?"

"That's Theodore and he doesn't like it either. Let me take your glass."

"Who is this?" Caleb pointed.

"That's Sam, the Spider Man."

"Don't you have *any girls?"* he asked. Coming from a family with four sisters, he had a hard time believing my plants weren't *girls* as well as *boys.*

"Sure, but Isabella, Matilda, and Geraldine all died of plant leprosy. All that are left are the boys!"

"What's that leopardsy?" the boy wanted to know, looking around for a huge jungle cat in the rich green leaves of the other plants. He didn't see one.

I told him about the powder that rotted away all their leafy arms and beautiful leaves. How did I know so much about indoor plants? Experience, time and attention. When I got too busy, I saw their leaves turn from green to gray without enough water. My small indoor jungle grew thicker when I pruned the plants, and when I offered vitamins, they developed more leaves and flowers.

My daily care of the plants is like God's care for us every day. He knows us even better than I know my plants! But while I forget to water sometimes, God always pays attention to our needs!

How have you leaned on God?

Further study: John 10:14-16

Day 4

You'll Never Be a Pest in God's Eyes!

Come, let us bow down in worship, let us kneel before the L*ORD our Maker.* Psalm 95:6

The seven-year-old proudly brought her pet in a fancy insect cage to show off at school.

"It's a caterpillar," Carlie explained. Then she told how this amazing creature would turn into a butterfly and look beautiful. She carefully held the squirming creature in her hand so all the class could pet its smooth, striped skin and let it curl with delight in their hands.

"I've been letting it sleep in its cage by my bed," she added.

There was a whole room full of "Ooos" and "Ahhhs" as the boys and girls moved forward to take a closer look. They thought they probably had seen something like this in the dirt before, but Carlie gave them reason to take a second look. How long before it turned into a butterfly? They all wanted to see!

Recognizing its special qualities, the children took the pet for a walk and picked fresh leaves for the caterpillar's afternoon snack. In the afternoon, Carlie and her friends said, "He's feeling so lonely! Just look at that sad face!" So they brought it out again for another round of petting and admiration.

Never had a pet had a life like this! Late in the day, I got a close look at Carlie's pet while it was sleeping. To the children, the creature was perfect. But I knew his type: this pampered creature was never going to change to a butterfly.

It was, in truth, a cutworm!

The cutworm is famous in gardening circles, taking first choice of juicy vegetable plants. Gentle gardeners everywhere premeditate its murder using poison, a trowel, a bucket of water, or a garden tiller. There's nothing left for even a decent burial.

How do I know? I'd done it, of course. If Carlie knew that "murderer" was stamped across my forehead, she'd never leave her pet with me for a minute.

Carlie would never allow any kind of bad end for her pet.

Nor would God wish bad for us. We are all precious creatures in his eyes. Even those of us who act like cutworms are unique and appreciated. In the same way that Carlie and the children loved and cared for their caterpillar, God cares for us.

God doesn't think of us as too stressed, too busy, or too sick to be loved. We're not! We are just what God wants: someone who is one of a kind and who is a custom-designed piece!

You deserve the best and he has it for you. Cutworms, slugs, and squash beetles may be the hungry, the bad, the ugly. They're part of God's universe. You are one, part of God's flock, never, ever to be left behind.

Further study: Genesis 1:26-27

Day 5

If You Love Someone, Belt it Out!

"Because he loves me," says the Lord, "I will rescue him; I will protect him, for he acknowledges my name. He will call upon me, and I will answer him. I will be with him in trouble, I will deliver him and honor him. With long life will I satisfy him and show him my salvation." Psalm 91:14-16

The jazz concert for my elementary students was a welcome change from practicing spelling, math and reading. As my students and I were seated, I felt a surprise coming on at my right elbow. Adam cupped his hands around his mouth. I reached out to stop whatever might be coming. With a smile that could light up a stadium, eight-year-old Adam stood and shouted, "I LOVE YOU!!" at the band. All five hundred sets of eyes turned to see where all that love was coming from. The other kids weren't surprised.

Flushed with embarrassment, I wondered what the right teacher thing might be to say. I whispered to Adam, "Saying 'I love you' is good, Adam, but it's better if you say it to one person and mean it." I remembered all of Adam's notes. He often told his family and friends he loved them. I tend to hold back. Adam is not in the "wait and see" school of love. Nor is God.

"Shouting in a crowd really takes a lot out of love, Adam," I lectured him. "Why don't you save it for a one-on-one with your friends?"

"I was saying it to just *one person*," he explained still beaming. "Look there next to the big drum! That's my cousin!"

How lucky are Adam's family members! They know he loves them, will stand by them, be proud of them, and listen to them with all his heart.

Imagine someone loving, protecting and promising to take care of you like Adam does with his friends and family.

There's already someone like that here for you and you're already in his family. That's a power higher than all of us, someone who never fails us, who provides for us and protects us. You are the picture-magnet on his refrigerator. You are in his brag-book. He knows your whole life ahead of time and cares about you anyway. God loves you!

Who in your life needs to hear that you love them? Belt out those powerful words!

Further study: Psalm 85:10-13

Day 6

You Sure Look Different with Your Clothes On!

The word of the L*ORD* *came to me saying, "Before I formed you in the womb I knew you, before you were born, I set you apart; I appointed you as a prophet to the nations.*" Jeremiah 1:5

Ron's shaggy blonde hair was cupped thick around his face when I saw him in the grocery store showcased against the European cheeses and deli meat. It was the first time to see him wearing something bigger than a hot mitt! He also looked at me with total surprise. I had never seen Ron with a shirt on. But then, he hadn't seen me with one on either.

He stared, then blurted. "You sure look different with your clothes on!"

I thought the same of him. Were we lovers, only meeting in a motel when our needs were greatest or is Ron a male model? Is he hopelessly stuck on himself and determined to show off his compact well-muscled, hairy body?

Well, no.

I never before saw him before without wet hair, and water dripping off his body. We swam laps in parallel lanes at the local pool for several summer seasons.

The world may cry for more skin and less clothes. Ron and I already had that at the Aquatic Center!

"You sure look different with your clothes on!" could have been the catch phrase of my life as mascot of the generation "If it feels good, do it."

Majoring in Fun 101, I sneered at my creator. "Hey, God, if you're out there, you can kill me off before I'm forty! I've done everything I wanted to do and it sucks!" Doing it my way most often left me with a stomach cramped with worry. God must have felt sad to see me choose so poorly, but he was patient. It took a lot to get my attention. Six thousand miles from home, I nearly lost my life on a dangerous solo adventure. The journey back to him had to come in baby steps. What is his plan for me? I'm still finding out.

God doesn't just know you inside and out, but he knows what talents he has given you. He knows how he wants you to use them. He knows every joyful event in your life as well as the disappointments, losses, awards, victories, and challenges ahead. God knows the length of your life and what he wants you to do with it.

No matter where you are with God right now, he has not given up on you. Your age doesn't matter, nor cellulite, moles, bitten fingernails, or the things you do best and worse.

You may not see the plan now, but God is smiling with his hidden agenda for your life. Will you let him advise and lead you? Wherever you are in your journey, God can take you there.

Who is God to you today?

Further study: 1 Samuel 16:1-13

Day 7

Who are Your Friends at This Hour?

Lord, you have been our dwelling place throughout all generations. Before the mountains were born or you brought forth the earth and the world, from everlasting to everlasting, you are God.

Psalm 90:1-2

You know who your friends are if you have to call them at 5:30 in the morning.

But I didn't want to call anyone. Twenty miles from home on a bicycle, I'd just have to struggle with the flat tire. During the last five flats, I changed the tube, sometimes pinched it in the rim, and it went flat again. I began to dread the bike wheel wobbling with a flat, even though I had a tube and pump.

Twice before, after a long walk that left my legs twitching with fatigue, I had stopped at my friend Mark's house. He had lifted the bike into his truck and took me home.

"I think I'll call you 'The Flat Tire Queen,'" he laughed.

Now, I wasn't anywhere near Mark or anyone else where country etiquette applies. Banging on a stranger's door only thirty minutes after sunup may be okay if someone is bleeding all over the porch, missing a family member, cattle or horses, or had been attacked by a wild animal. A flat tire is no such emergency.

"Curses on those goat heads!" I pulled two out of the front tire. The tire was still flat. "This is really too long of a walk," I thought. "Lord, please send someone to pick me up as soon as possible!" I lay the bike down and waited. Fat chance of traffic at this hour! There wasn't a car in sight from here to South America.

The rolling hills waved with the rhythm of golden wildflowers lit in the slanting sun. Nothing was going to happen quickly.

The scene wrapped around me like an embrace. I could feel the presence of God, his peace and his time.

Forget about someone bailing me out. I had to take responsibility for the tire.

Like a parent, God guided me through the repair. With only a little struggle with the flat tube, I mounted a new one. It held air! God kept his arms around me all the way home through the country roads, and he gave me the greatest gift of all: learning to help myself.

God proves he is the friend there for all times without boundaries, even thirty minutes after sunup.

What circumstances have pushed you into leaning on God and yourself?

Further study: Job 5:17-24

Questions

Which Button Do You Push to Get God to Come Out?

Who is God to you at this point in your life?

____

____

____

____

Give an example of God in your or someone else's life.

____

____

____

____

What can you do for yourself today in thoughts and action to appreciate the gift you are from God?

____

____

____

____

____

Predict how much change there would be if you bombarded someone with love for six months who seemed to be unlovable?

____

____

____

____

Reflections:

____

____

____

____

____

____

Some people want an affidavit from
God that he really exists.

Danny Thomas

Week 2

Is This Heart-Thumping Terror or Just Another Monday?

Day 1

Heart-Thumping Terror in Everyday Life and the 100% Proven Cure

When I am afraid, I will trust in you. In God, whose word I praise, in God I trust; I will not be afraid. What can mortal man do to me? Psalm 56:3-4

Her head was buzzing with fatigue and she was seeing stars by the time Sandra arrived home from a Women's Prayer Conference. It had been a long and sleepy four-hour drive. Now it was 2:30 a.m. The night was dark and moonless. Her husband was sleeping soundly.

As she entered the house quietly through the side door, Sandra tiptoed down the hall into the bedroom so she wouldn't wake Jim, her husband.

She set her suitcase down gently in the dark. Then Sandra felt around for something she needed desperately—toothpaste! She closed her hand around the tube. Now she would be able to end this long day and go to bed with clean teeth. She went to the bathroom without turning on the light, squeezed the contents onto her toothbrush, and started brushing.

Immediately, Sandra knew it wasn't toothpaste! It was greasy. No fresh mint taste, either. It tasted like medicine. Yuck! Sandra snapped on the light, and then realized with a shock what the tube was: cream for clearing a yeast infection. She spit it out and kept spitting. Sandra hoped and prayed that it wasn't too late! Jim slept on. He had no clue his wife's life might be in danger, and she wasn't going to wake him.

Even though it was now 2:30 in the morning, Sandra picked up the phone to call her close friend, wife of the local pharmacist. She told her about the greasy paste and what she had done.

"Ask Mel if I'm going to be okay!"

Sally nudged her husband until he groaned. Mel's sleepy reply was, "Tell her she won't have to worry about yeast infections in her MOUTH for a long time!"

God is there for us in all hours of our need. It can be everyday challenges or life-threatening needs. Fear is not God's answer, but can be as common in our everyday life as a hiccup. His is assurance that no matter what you give to him, he will handle it. We can think of no solutions, but he can. When you are afraid, can you turn the challenge over to God?

Further study: 1 Peter 3:13-15

Day 2
Murder She Read

You will not fear the terror of night, nor the arrow that flies by day. Psalms 91:5

Murder? Definitely, it was a possibility as well as a great plot. Who would suspect that gentle Jeane had blood clotted on her coffee tables, knives in the bathroom, and murder weapons next to her bed? How many skeletons would the police find buried under the white-haired widow's two struggling tomato plants?

None. Only rocks and roots were buried in my widowed mother's yard. These plots, murders, and deadly instruments were between the pages of her many who-dun-its.

Jeane seemed to do a good job of separating her reading for fun from real life—except for once. When I called to tell her I'd be out of town for a week for leadership training, Mom responded absently, "Uh-huh." I might have guessed she stopped to answer the phone while reading yet another book with a skull on the spine. She had read every mystery in the libraries in two counties where she split her time, summer and winter.

While she became an expert in sabotage, cover-up and unraveling a mystery, I left work and headed down the mountains on wet dark roads.

Anxious to get out of the mountains before the roads turned icy, I thought,

"I'd better skip my usual cappuccino. I don't have time."

Just a little sleep the night before didn't go far. Sometimes I couldn't tell the wide winding road from the shoulders. But there wasn't a coffee for sixty more miles.

“Maybe a snack will help,” I thought, waving my free hand in a picnic chest. Instead of an apple, I banged my hand into a box. It was powdered cappuccino coffee mix! God knew just what I needed. With a swig of water, the mix became instant coffee. Quickly, I came back to life and was alert enough to drive safely the rest of the journey.

Until I got home a week later, I didn’t know Mom had started leaving messages on my answering machine at my house the first day. The first beep was, “Jo, why don’t you join me for dinner tonight? I’m making clams in white sauce, your favorite. Let me know!” The second, “Thought you’d enjoy a meatloaf! Come on over about six!” By the time five days had gone by, the messages were shorter and more like, “Jo, where are you? I haven’t been able to reach you for five days! I’m beginning to worry!”

When I returned home and called Mom, she let out a noisy sigh. “I’m so relieved! I checked your house after I couldn’t find you for three days! Your bedding was twisted and pulled off on the floor! I thought someone might have kidnapped you! I was ready to call the police!”

Any other mother might have remarked, “You didn’t make your bed before you left!”

Mom had sleuthed like Miss Marple, tip-toeing through my house looking for clues, murder weapons, blood, body parts, or signs of a struggle.

Even though the only danger was foul weather and not foul play, both Mom and I were reassured that God takes care of us, our fears, and our needs.

Do you have a worry that you can give to him today?

Further study: Matthew 8:23-27

Day 3
Danger in the Wilderness

Even though I walk through the valley of the shadow of death, I will fear no evil, for you are with me; your road and your staff, they comfort me. Psalm 23:4

Tension was high that summer in Flagstaff, Arizona. Nine-year-old Jennifer Wilson had been riding her bike down a Forest Service Road, and then the girl and her bicycle disappeared. Now, it was the nineteenth day since she was missing. Churches united for a week of prayer. Several hundred volunteers planned to canvas the town and surrounding area that weekend.

Still, because camping was as natural to us as pancakes for breakfast, I packed for a weekend getaway with the boys, not yet eight. Summer college classes had been intense. Camping always restored our souls. I had planned to be far enough away from the search that no one would bother us.

A faint, two-track trail led up an incline to a sheltered forest area. It was a perfect campsite! When morning came, steady traffic of four wheel drives, pick-ups, and sport utility vehicles rumbled down the dirt road below, part of the search, I guessed.

Then, an ancient station wagon, red with dust, rattled to a stop at the bottom on my hill, I could see it through the aspens, but I knew they couldn't see me or our hidden campsite. I heard the murmur of voices above the sounds of the forest, and then heavy breathing and footsteps as the driver and his middle-aged heavyset woman steadily strode up my hill. Their hair was uncombed and dull with dirt.

When they spotted me, the man's first words were ominous, "Are you all *alone* out here?" He emphasized the word "alone." Both were dressed in worn, dirty clothes. My gut feeling was that we all were in danger.

I began praying, and knew I couldn't show my fear.

"No, of course we're not alone out here," I replied cheerfully. "The rest of our family is over there picking up pine cones." My sons were children. I was an unarmed woman a long way from town.

The man stepped so close I could smell his foul breath. As he spat out these words, I felt his breath on my face. "Don't you know it's dangerous out here? That little girl is still missing and there are wild animals out here."

"Yeah, I know," I told them. "That's sad about the girl. It's so hard on her family not knowing what happened." There was a long pause. I continued praying silently.

Then something in the couple's expression changed, from a hard stare to a quizzical look. I didn't dare take my eyes off them to see what it was they saw just behind me.

"Well, we got to be going. We thought we'd warn you."

For over a mile, I could hear the old car clattering, the danger leaving with them. What had they seen in the forest behind me? I scanned the trees. No one. I will always believe the couple saw an angel who stepped out of the forest just in time, looking like a brawny lumberjack with an axe in his hands.

There is great power and protection in our God. We can count on it.

How has God protected you?

Further study: 1 Samuel 24:1-13

Day 4

The Benchmark Birthday Plunge

> *...But Jesus was sleeping. The disciples went and woke him, saying, "Lord, save us! We're going to drown!" He replied, "You of little faith, why are you so afraid?" Then he got up and rebuked the winds and the waves, and it was completely calm.*
>
> Matthew 8:24-26

What had I gotten myself into? I was surrounded by a locker room full of buck naked women of all sizes and shapes. Obviously, they weren't bashful. Not only was every one of them more buxom than I was, but they could swim fearlessly!

"Come on, Russell!" I told myself. "This is a benchmark birthday and it's about time you got over your fear of water!" When my birthdays end with a "0," I call it a benchmark and force myself to do something new. This year, it was to get over my fear of deep water, so I enrolled in a Master's Swim Class.

I pushed through the steamy door to the inside pool lanes.

Could you imagine the disciples refusing to get in the fishing boat because they couldn't touch or see the bottom of the lake? That wouldn't be a hurdle at the pool. Gosh, I could see the black lines all the way to the other side!

When Coach began, he taught us from where we were. Lydia zoomed by me, doing fancy flip turns at the end of the lane. Roger lapped me, and I was the one wearing Zoomer fins! Cindy churned through the water and I never saw her come up for air! Coach told me later that when I started, I swam like a drowning cockroach!

"Jo, don't worry about the flip turns," Coach assured me, kneeling by my lane. "Let's just work on keeping your face in the water. You're not going to drown. Come up for a breath every three strokes. Can you do that?" I did.

As time went on, I swam faster and enjoyed the rhythm of swimming and varied work outs. I was no longer afraid of the water. Time in the lanes let me relax and think.

Jesus scolded the disciples for being so afraid. When he calmed the waves, the disciples were stunned with Jesus' power. I'm not surprised at the power of God, for he calms the wakes and my fear of our local swimming pool.

What storm can Jesus calm in your life today?

Further study: Isaiah 35:3-4

Day 5

Have You Gathered at the River?

So do not fear, for I am with you; do not be dismayed, for I am your God. I will strengthen you and help you; I will uphold you with my righteous right hand.

Isaiah 41:10

It is so wild on the river in Alaska, you can have a barbeque with friends and nearly all of them have hairy paws the size of catchers' mitts. This was day three of a four-day raft trip, and it was midnight. Someone was knocking on the door of my tent. I was relieved he wasn't wearing fur!

It was only Lance, my son, warning me there was trouble.

"What?! Why?!" I sat up awake.

"Tomorrow you and Trent might have to walk in the river beside the raft. The bladders of my raft burst. We can't fix it." Sure enough, it was flat as a pillowcase.

He and his brother, Travis, had worked as professional raft guides for several years and made the wild river trip a dozen times, sometimes handling emergencies. This time, the trip was just for fun. Five of us had rafted safely through calm water and rapids, rocks, and rain.

I cried, "I can't walk in the river! If I slip and fall with this bad knee, I can be crippled for life!" My whining made my son's forehead crinkle with worry.

"We'll work as a team, Mom."

"Of course," I thought, "and that team will include God." I began praying.

The next morning, Travis and his wife, Maria, packed all the gear on his small raft. It was dangerously overloaded, but still afloat. The second flat raft had to carry three of us out.

Lance attached a pump to the bladders and coached Trent while the novice rower worked. "Good job, Trent! You're a natural at this! When we go on the next trip, I'll teach you to go through the rapids!" From his encouragement, we began to forget that there were only inches between us and a freezing river, and that Lance never stopped pumping air into the bladders. Cold fingers of rain wrapped around us. With my rubber boots dangling in the cold water, I continued to pray.

Then I noticed the raft didn't lose any more air and the water was so calm and shallow I could see the rocks on the bottom. It seemed like a couple of muscled angels were holding up the raft. So far, none of us had even gotten our feet wet!

After an hour and a half of Lance pumping, Trent rowing, and the rain misting over us, Trent guided the raft to a Forest Service camp at the edge of the water.

When the Forest Service worker stepped out of the trees, his full trimmed beard touched each shoulder in a half circle. He called out cheerfully, "What can I do for you?" While the men talked, the tethered raft sighed and the rear end eased under the water until it lay on the bottom.

Filling the rescue boat with the ruined raft and all the heavy gear from the two rafts, the ranger took Lance and me aboard. Trent rode out with Travis and Maria. As the power boat lurched to speed, Lance braced his arm across me to protect me. It was much like what God had done, bracing us against danger in the wilderness, miraculously holding up the raft until we could get help, and getting us all safely back to the take-out point without even needing a Band-aid. That because He's a powerful and caring God!

Getting back to the take-out point first, Lance and I had all the coolers of food with us while we waited for the three to row in. Anyone want a cookie?

Further study: 1 Samuel 19:1-10

Day 6

In My Heart, There is a Melody!

I sought the Lord, and he answered me; he delivered me from all my fears. Psalm 34:4

Some people would rather die than give a speech. What else is on the list of most popular fears? Water, spiders, dentists, buying a car, relapse, collapse, and snakes.

Amy thought about her and others' fears. "Where does singing a solo for the first time fit in?" she wondered.

She was doing okay at first, and Choir Director Ed smiled seeing his star pupil reach out with her lovely voice so crisp that every word of the message was clear.

Amy was all confidence, and then her voice wobbled and stopped. The choir director followed her glance. Amy was staring at the whole family of four-part harmonizers: three daughters, a son, and a husband, and in the center was Mrs. Professional Voice Coach. While the melody-line singers at the church struggled with black spots in front of their eyes—the music notes—Voice Coach's family broke out in four-part harmony that they read right out of the song book! Next to a nest of birds, there wasn't any family to whom singing was more natural.

Choir director Ed had spent months encouraging Amy, remembering during her audition, as she hid behind the baby grand and was no more audible than a squeaky pet toy. To Ed mouthing, "Go on! Go on!" the pause seemed longer than the time it takes for a jury to agree on a verdict. Amy signaled the pianist and began again with strength, and confidence. A solo would never be so frightening for her again. She had forged on through something that felt worse than death itself. Amy's fear still shook her, but she realized Mrs. Professional Voice Coach was not frowning at her, but smiling and nodding. Amy was able to smile.

God gives us new situations that are beyond our experience and understanding at the time. He expands our circle and our world that way. As we grow, the circle grows.

It is God's way of shaping us into an even more competent woman!

What new skill can you ask God to help you try?

Further study: Psalm 27:1

Day 7

What is Scritch-Scratching on the Tent?

If you make the Most High your dwelling—even the LORD, who is my refuge—then no harm will befall you, no disaster will come near your tent. Psalm 91:9-10

Bob's beautiful new wife, Glenda, loved the outdoors. While dating, they hiked and biked together, enjoyed long walks holding hands, and now that they had their place together, they had added backyard barbeques to their outdoor activities.

Bob and his parents, siblings, and his cousins all liked roughing it. "Do it in a tent" was the family slogan. Bob guessed he might even have been conceived in a nylon-sided home! Even though Glenda was raised in a city, he was sure she would love it too. This was the moment!

"Let's go camping this weekend. The weather is beautiful and sunny. We can even try out the Dutch oven!"

"Oh, Honey, I'd love it! Did you rent a motor home for us?"

"No, Sweetie Cakes, but I borrowed Dad's little tent camper. It's small and cozy, just right for cuddling!"

She agreed, not grasping entirely what it means to "rough it." They packed the small sedan, hooked on the little trailer and drove until nearly dark. Everything was romantic as they prepared the evening meal on a camp stove as the setting sun lit their excited faces.

The trouble started when it came time for bed. They lay comfortably inside the camper that was only big enough for the two of them. Glenda chose the place closest to the door. "I love the smell of the land and the clean air," Bob murmured as he drifted off with his lovely Glenda in his arms, but she couldn't sleep. Glenda listened fearfully to the night noises that were a lullaby to Bob.

Suddenly, scritch-scratch! Scritch-scratch!

"Bob, wake up! Something is scratching on our tent! What can it be?"

Bob decided to omit mentioning any of the large animals who made their home in the area, such as muscled mountain lions or nasty-tempered javelina, so he just said, "Probably something small like a raccoon."

"I'm scared. Could you see what it is?"

So Bob climbed over Glenda, her body stiff with fear and gazed around in the silver moonlight. "It's nothing, Glenda. Let's go back to sleep. It's a beautiful night!"

Scritch-scratch! Scritch-scratch! Scritch-scratch! The sound persisted and Glenda interrupted Bob's soft breathing.

"Bob, do you hear that? Something is still scratching on our tent!"

Again, he sleepily sat up, climbed over Glenda, and checked outside. Everything was in place. No animal tracks either that he could see. A gentle breeze had come up, and it was as if God's hand was waving a welcome.

Bob had only sighed himself to sleep again when Glenda woke him with her frightened request to check again!

"This is the last time I check! Nothing is out there! No tracks or anything! Go to sleep, Sweetheart. I'll hold you. We're safe here."

The sun kissed Bob awake and he groggily climbed over sleeping Glenda to stretch and start the hot water for morning cocoa.

It was then Bob himself heard the scritch-scratch! He looked all around and finally found it—the nylon ties for the tent windows! With the gentle breeze, the ties had scraped the tent walls all night.

All that fear was for nothing! When Glenda got up, they laughed together about it.

How often do we fear that something will happen, and in truth, it never does. Worry, anxiety, and fear can be rolled up into a common idea: a waste of time.

God has our life and our fears handled if we let him.

Compare how you and God look at fear. Which way seems better?

Further study: Matthew 6:25-34

Questions

Is This Heart-Thumping Terror or Just Another Monday?

Reflect on experiences that have made you feel fearful. Did you handle all of them turning your fear to God?

How would you compare his handling of your fears to your own management?

What specific fears would you like to turn over to God today?

Reflections:

We are continually faced
with a series of great opportunities
brilliantly disguised as insoluble problems.

John W. Gardner

Week 3

Is Red Your Natural Face Color?

Day 1

Seth's Secret for Making Work More Fun

Do not offer the parts of your body to sin, as instruments of wickedness, but rather offer yourselves to God, as those who have been brought from death to life; and offer the parts of your body to him as instruments of righteousness. For sin shall not be your master, because you are not under law, but under grace.

Romans 6:13-14

"Since Moses came, I haven't had a day off for the last seventeen days!"

The muscled teen was knee deep in mud under a cloudless sky bleached white by a desert sun.

"Yeah," agreed another sweaty worker mixing mud for bricks. "We can't even use straw now with the adobe bricks. I'd say that the real problem around here is management! They don't understand what it takes to do the job!

"That's right!" a tanned older man quipped as he angrily slung mud into a form.

"He's interfering with my benefits! I don't like it! Since all the fish died because Moses turned the Nile to blood, I haven't been able to grill even one tilapia!"

"And how do they expect us to raise gardens for food when we don't have any time off while the sun is up?"

"And they keep cutting staff so we have four times as much to do with more lashes. The new managers are whipping crosshatch patterns on my back! They even refuse to let us go home early in bad sandstorms!"

"Just how do they expect the women and seniors to build all these pyramids? There's no respect around here!"

Then Seth came along for his shift, his loud jolly voice singing a joyful song. He took the heavy clay bricks out of the molds and stacked them neatly.

"That figures," complaining Korah mumbled. "He's only been married a week and a slave in this outfit for just a few weeks. Give him time."

But they did give him time. Seth continued to joyfully praise God and said, "I'm glad to have a job in these hard times. I have food, a wonderful wife and God, and I'm getting a good tan!"

Zooming forward about 3,500 years, this is the kind of conversation we might hear in any employee lounge. Are we going to be a Korah or a Seth?

I had to ask myself that very question. When my company came out the lowest in the region on employee morale, I gloated at first, "Now maybe they'll change this…"

Then I stopped as my ears burned. I realized that with my complaining, I was part of the low spirits. It certainly undid my pledge to God and fellow employees to lift them with words, to give gift baskets for those fighting illness, and to bake cookies for the staff now and then. All that was for nothing the second I said, "The real problem around here is…."

I failed to control my tongue. It's a small part of the body, but more powerful and damaging than a fire fanned by the wind. A tongue rattling on can overtake friendships, kill love, cause families or groups to argue and split, and build walls taller than the highest mountain in the galaxy.

Seth had the real answer: controlling his tongue and his attitude.

Jesus wants us to build bridges, not walls. How well do we do that?

Further study: Ephesians 4:29-32

Day 2

Sin is a Three-Letter Word

Good and upright is the Lord; therefore he instructs sinners in his ways. He guides the humble in what is right and teaches them his way. Psalm 25:8-9

Kindergarten teacher, Mrs. Layden, had worked an extra hour to prepare a science activity so it would go smoothly. But small children, like all other sized people, can be unpredictable. Some are more unpredictable than others.

Mrs. Layden noticed that as she led the class into the room, Jeremy fell out of one of his unfastened shoes. He sprawled on the floor, and then scrambled to reach and find the other shoe.

The teacher had a smile in her voice as she announced, "You're going to find some fun things in the middle of your tables, but..." she paused for emphasis, "I don't want you to touch them!"

The pint-sized five-year-olds bubbled with excitement as they sat at their tables. They didn't know what to do with their hands! Each group looked at the colorful toys, paper, and craft tools with awe! The boys and girls all wanted to talk all at once.

Meanwhile, Jeremy, now with two shoes, skipped around the room with joy and said, "Hey! We're going to find some fun things in the middle of our tables!!!"

He couldn't stop himself! Jeremy touched a plastic dinosaur! "Wow, this is made from the same stuff as my walking hands that go down the wall!" he announced. Jeremy wound up like a pitcher, ready to throw that dinosaur at the window to see if it would somersault down the glass.

The teacher cleared her throat. With a weapon that makes educators famous worldwide, she lasered him a look that would melt aluminum. Jeremy dropped the toy and hung his head. Busted!

"Jeremy, I care so much about you. But I'm sad you didn't listen.

Let's try again to do better." She still loved him. Someday when Jeremy was all grown up, Mrs. Layden would see him again and remember that sometimes she had to take aspirin just because of him. Looking at a grown-up Jeremy, she would hear that he worked hard and took good care of his wife and children. He had become a great dad. His shoes were always fastened!

Teachers often remember a "problem child" more than less challenging people in their lives. After all, it wasn't just Jeremy touching the dinosaurs that spurred her memory, but when he ate his boogers instead of using a tissue, cried when he couldn't find his turquoise crayon, and when he asked questions in the middle of the moment of silence during the flag raising ceremony. He stood out.

Jeremy was a lot of trouble. Lots of us are a bother, too. But to God, we're worth all the attention and shaping. It takes a lot of tries. The little Jeremy and the grown-up version both deserve love and hugs from someone who believes in them.

Over and over, God's chosen people, the Israelites, made bad mistakes, were sorry, came back to God, then left him again.

Like Jeremy, my words and actions had gotten me into trouble the week before. I was no different than he was throwing a sticky dinosaur against the window.

The Israelites provided lots of headaches for God. But God never stopped loving them—or us.

What can we change to do better today?

Further study: Matthew 18:12-14

Day 3
Longing for Lawn Chairs

> *You shall not covet your neighbor's house. You shall not covet your neighbor's wife, or his manservant or maidservant, his ox or donkey, or anything that belongs to your neighbor.* Exodus 20:17

Four child-sized plastic lawn chairs, one loveseat, and five adult-sized plastic chairs held a special place in my neighbor's yard ever since the summer when Henry, Marie, and family moved in with Henry's mom.

Sometimes I found myself feeling jealous. My patio chairs were heavy-duty, color coordinated with thick cushions that made them as comfortable as living room furniture.

With a work schedule as unpredictable as the weather and my grown children and their families living far away, my chairs were empty most of the time unless a stray cat jumped the fence.

The neighbor's lawn chairs themselves were not what I longed for. I envied the relationships. Their plastic furniture was full of family members every weekend. Their laughter and barbequed burgers make everyone in the neighborhood smile. Compared to Grandma Margaret's where four generations shared experiences and closeness, my home seemed empty.

Exodus 20 states God's original commands to Moses and the people. In modern terms, it might read, "Thou shalt not covet your neighbor's husband or significant other, vacuum cleaner or dishwasher, newer truck or car than yours, or anything that belongs to your neighbor—like his lawn chairs."

Suddenly, I remembered that Henry and Marie moved there because their dream home they'd spent years building had been taken by the bank. The four generations together were making the best of their world imploding. When the housing market crashed and Henry's construction business slowed to a crawl, Henry and Marie lost their home.

These ancient guidelines in Exodus 20 give us the best tools for life. How can we apply them to our thinking, choices and actions?

Focusing on God and a relationship with him far exceeds focusing on lawn chairs.

Where is your focus today?

Further study: Ecclesiastes 2:10-11; John 14:15

Day 4

The 100-yard Chapel Sprint

Come to me, all you who are weary and burdened, and I will give you rest. Take my yoke upon you and learn from me, for I am gentle and humble in heart, and you will find rest for your souls.

Matthew 11:28-29

According to caring dog trainers, good canine behavior starts with simple commands: "Come," "Sit," "Stay" and "Heel." The last command is translated "behaves sensibly on a leash." Fletcher, the basset hound, towed us around the block like a lawn tractor. He bolted to strangers for a treat. He followed his nose to places where no dog had ever been. He was, most of the time, lovable, but sometimes disobedient.

In the summer church camp where our little family lived and worked, we welcomed Christian Motorcyclist Association members as guests one weekend.

As I drove up to our tiny log cabin, Fletcher looked around at the eighty-two wooded acres. He decided it was too cramped for his style. Instead of jumping out of the truck and heading for the door, he bolted into the trees, heading for music and people who would love his sad eyes and smooth coat. Petting and snacks were guaranteed with this crowd.

"Travis, catch Fletcher! Run!" The lanky twelve-year-old sprinted along a dirt path after the dog, but without a leash. His first strategy was to check behind the cafeteria where the staff tossed leftovers on the slope, like sandwiches and waffles. Fletcher loved to lick up leftovers, and Travis found him there. Not for long. The powerful muscled dog pulled away from the boy at a run as his legs churned to the wide open chapel doors. Fletcher's ears twirled like batons. He barked in joyful rhythm to the music inside, and then dashed down the aisle. As he whirled around and headed to the open door, the dog stopped for a moment.

Just then I drove up in the truck with the leash. Dangling his favorite snack, a piece of bread, out the window, I shouted, "Here, Fletcher!" At last, obedience! He followed his nose to the truck.

Someone laughed, "That dog must be an evangelist!"

Even though the dog flunked some commands, God used Fletcher as several came to the altar that day chuckling. It was a time anyone could change their heart and life with Jesus, and humor nudged each along.

Have you relaxed and let Jesus guide you His way?

Further study: Psalm 34:8-11

Day 5

Will All The Accused Please Line Up?

> *Remember, O* Lord*, your great mercy and love, for they are from of old. Remember not the sins of my youth and my rebellious ways; according to your love remember me, for you are good, O* Lord.
>
> Psalm 25: 6-7

The one-stoplight town where I live is quiet. Sometimes, too quiet.

Do you ever feel like you just have to break the rules?

I felt that way one Sunday. Who would notice anyway? So the first thing I did totally on purpose was to run the stop sign in front of my house. A block away, when I got to the next stop sign that opened onto a more traveled road, I just eased around the corner without using a turn signal and without stopping. There wasn't even a cricket crossing the road, and definitely no cars, tractors, bicycles, or tumbleweeds moseying toward the intersection.

Next, I turned onto a minor highway shown in double digits on the state map. Did I stop? Nope. I just oozed around the corner to the post office, a gathering place because there is no home mail delivery. The sign in front of the post office read, "NO PARKING ANY TIME." I looked both ways, and then parked there anyway. About the time I opened the driver's door, a car came into view and went whizzing around my truck, ripe for ripping off the driver's door.

By morning, I hadn't gotten over my rebellion, and was gleeful I hadn't been caught. Driving before dawn to work, I was startled with a blast of red light as bright as lightning. I squinted, and then remembered what it meant. This would cost me as much as two new tires. Now my face and photo were in the archives of the Speeders' Hall of Fame.

I had forgotten that the towns in our area recently added five sets of cameras to make sure all of us drove nicely. It has been a great money-maker so far. There could be no arguing, seeing a mug shot of a grown woman old enough to know better. The wide-brimmed hat gave me away completely.

My silly rebellious behavior was like a teen saying, "I'm not going to do it!" just because it has the letters N-O in it.

Following God's laws is part of what God expects of us. Loving God and following His law sets us apart. Not accepting His rules resembles my thumbing my nose at traffic signs. We are always caught. Fortunately, we know the judge.

Based on God's expectations, how can you improve your attitude about authority?

Further study: Exodus 19

Day 6

Where the Rubber Meets the Road

Blessed is the man who always fears the L*ORD, but he who hardens his heart falls into trouble.*

Proverbs 28:14

"I shouldn't, but I will," I thought as I handed the car keys, the keys for *our only car,* to my sixteen-year-old twin sons to practice driving. Normally, the twins walked everywhere they wanted to go, the soles of their rubber sneakers pounding the pavement, including eight miles round trip to school.

Today, I felt like a wilted, middle-aged mom as I hung weakly onto the doorway of the barn-red house. Swaying from the effort of standing after having surgery on my bottom a few days before, I had only one logical thought in mind: to lie down. All other thoughts of wisdom and my to-do list whirled away like a dust devil on this warm summer day.

Two-and-a-half acres of land around the country house gave the drivers a circular dirt driveway and trails for practice.

"Don't worry Mom," Travis grinned confidently. "I can teach Lance." This lanky boy had been bouncing over two-track roads for weeks with me while his look-alike brother had been doing time in summer school. He had gobs of experience! Twenty-seven miles total!

Everything for me was fuzzy as the tall twins strode confidently to the truck.

Soon, the sound of the truck roaring over the roads gave me and the neighbors the idea that all was well in their souls and the dirt driveway. I lay on the sofa with a pillow under my rear. Everything sounded normal—for a while.

Then there was silence: no clacketa of an engine. I listened long and hard. Nothing. The twins stood at the door. There was no blood. But also, there was no truck. They pointed at each other starting to talk at the same time.

"Mom, I told Lance to stop, but he hit this cedar," driving coach Travis explained. "The truck looks okay, though."

Dragging along with dread, I scanned the landscape for the truck. A cedar was jammed against the door. When I turned the key, I prayed the truck was still alive. It coughed, then started. As I backed out, I noticed the hood was buckled. Its appearance was only the forerunner of the ways the truck was never the same again. Now it took two people to open the hood.

Another day, another dent. One twin explained, "Did you know that a log jumped up and hit the side of the truck?" Then a short errand to the grocery store two miles away turned into a half-day adventure. The phone call started with the question, "Could you call Chris to help get the truck out of the wash?" I took back my keys forever.

Now there was a whole new meaning for the tall teens when it came to "rubber meeting the road." It was the sound of their rubber sneakers once again taking them everywhere they wanted to go.

Parents forgive their kids and God forgives his, but there are consequences for every action that affect the future. Just as I was disappointed with the damage to the truck, God is sad with some of our choices.

My sons grew up to be safe, accident-free drivers, but in their own vehicles.

God lets us learn through our mistakes as we experience the consequences. No matter what happens, God still loves you!

How have you realized God's love for you?

Further study: 2 Samuel 12:1-14

Day 7

The Roar of the Stream, The Smell of Black Boxers

Humility and fear of the Lord bring wealth and honor and life. Proverbs 22:4

Being the only adult in the family is something like being a dictator. What you say goes. Having doubts isn't an option with so much responsibility in a family.

But there is a time to be humble—when we are wrong. It's good for us.

Clean socks on the passenger window of the station wagon flapped in the wind as I drove the kids back from a trip to see family in San Francisco. The compact wagon bulged with so much camping gear, food and essentials for the four-year-old twins, my teen nephew, and me, I couldn't see out the back window.

There wasn't much room for souvenirs like Ghirardelli chocolate and sour dough bread, so the boys got creative.

Traveling home through southern California, we all noticed a very strong odor in the area of nephew Chris in the passenger seat. Chris smelled his armpits. The twins did, too.

I couldn't help myself. "Chris, I know we camped last night. Did you change your underwear?" I thought of the teen's favorite black boxers. Somehow, they missed going in the washing machine nearly every load. Every time, he insisted "I've got plenty to wear in my backpack."

The thirteen-year-old peered at me with a disgusted look. "I DO have on clean underwear, why?"

When I stopped the car for the night at our mountain campsite, the boys sprung from the car like they were slung from a slingshot. I expected the smell to go with them. It didn't.

Then I discovered the stash of brown-and-serve sourdough bread under Chris's seat. I felt a rush of heat flow over me when I thought of confronting Chris. I begged his forgiveness. He did and we were a family again.

All the way home, the car smelled like dirt and pine cones, and I remembered how healing it is to be humble instead of right.

Hurting someone may be just through a look, an attitude, or in words. It's always worth it to make things right before driving off into the sunset.

Who needs to hear your apology today?

Further study: Psalm 25:15

Questions

Is Red Your Natural Face Color?

How would you evaluate yourself in accepting responsibility for your choices past, present, and future?

Break down areas of your own weakness and what changes are needed to make things right?

Reflections:

Phyllis McGinley writes, "Sin has always been an ugly word, but it has been made so in a new sense over the last half century. It has been made not only ugly, but passé. People are no longer sinful. They are only immature or underprivileged or frightened or, more particularly, sick." *

One of the heaviest burdens
a person can carry is a chip on his shoulder.

Olin Miller

*Phillips' Treasury of Humorous Quotations

Week 4

Count Your Blessings, Even When the Toilet is Overflowing!

Day 1

Count Your Blessings, Even When the Toilet is Overflowing!

> *Finally, brothers, whatever is true, whatever is noble, whatever is right, whatever is pure, whatever is lovely, whatever is admirable—if anything is excellent or praiseworthy—think about such things.*
>
> Philippians 4:8

"If you're going to add anything to your house," the realtor told me, "you need another bathroom, not a mural, patio, pool, shed, garage or outdoor spa. One bathroom is obsolete."

That advice never hit home until one Christmas Eve when one guest out of sixteen came to me with, "Aunt Jo, something is wrong with the toilet. We can't get it to flush. I really have to go!"

Was my toilet the new-fangled kind that is taller, with a trap as big as a python that can flush down bowling balls and never clog up? I peered down at the liquid and toilet paper mixed together like egg drop soup. No such luck.

While my brother Tony, whose passion is cooking, organized and filled numerous prep bowls in the kitchen for a feast and the house filled with wonderful smells, I tried plunging the toilet and using my usual tricks. Soon the water eased over the edge like a fountain, wetting my tennies.

"Mom, how is your toilet working over there?" I asked when I called her. "Can you handle a few more flushes?" Usually, her summer home nearby was locked up until May, but we'd heated and opened it for this special large Christmas reunion. There were three families at Mom's house, three at mine, and one at a motel.

She, like me, had the obsolete one-bathroom model home.

"Not very well, Jo. I might have to call a plumber, even though it's late!"

"Jo, I really have to go to the bathroom!" Betsy, my sister-in-law, pleaded. "What do you want us to do?"

"Give me a few minutes. I'll figure it out!"

"I have an announcement!" I gathered everyone around. "The boys and men will use the empty snowy field outside the fence as an outhouse. The women and girls will use this large soup pot, which we will clean thoroughly between uses. In the meantime, I'm calling a plumber! Any questions?"

Just mentioning the makeshift bathroom challenges brought out the urge to go.

Soon the guests in line at the soup pot and the field were relieved. Many were happy playing games while Chef Tony, wrapped in a full-length professional apron, fixed a fabulous feast. Everything and everyone was working well together except the toilet.

It was 4:00 p.m. by now. The plumber was thrilled to hear from me on Christmas Eve. When he arrived, he cheerfully remarked it was late enough; he'd have to charge for the holiday. Whistling and humming, he was full of songs of the season.

The toilet was working, and then I realized what a blessing all of it was that all of us were there together for the first time. The warm house was bursting with laughter, friends and family.

Some were toasting marshmallows in the fireplace, a novelty to all.

Home, food, family, friends, laughter. What more perfect gifts can God give us?

Further study: Deuteronomy 28:1-2

Day 2

Food is Fundamental

Taking the five loaves and the two fish and looking up to heaven, he gave thanks and broke the loaves. Then he gave them to the disciples, and the disciples gave them to the people. They all ate and were satisfied..."

Matthew 14:19-20

"Don't cut that applesauce cake yet, Lance!" Travis grabbed a building square and marked the centerline to make sure they would each get their equal share. Then each twin ate half of the homemade cake. They were satisfied, at least for thirty minutes or so. Unlike Jesus' feeding of the 5,000 men, there were no scraps left.

Now that my sons were teens, I found the only way to get their attention was with food. We got home from a camping trip and one of the two with the dirtiest face proclaimed, "I'm clean enough and I'm not going to take a shower!"

"That's too bad, Sweetie. There are fifteen pieces of hot French toast on the table and you won't be eating any of them." I heard the shower running immediately.

While other parents worried about their children getting into trouble with the law, I just had to deal with two athletic active, young men who burned off calories by the thousands as they bicycled, hiked, ran and walked long distances.

I tried a food cache under the bed. They found it. I moved the stash to the closet. Again, the teens poked around until they found it.

"Why are we having pancakes for dinner again, Mom? When can we get something decent to eat around here?" One of my offspring demanded.

"What happened to the olives?" I asked, picturing the twins eating olives off their fingers.

"Oh, them."

"What about the canned hash?" Travis's favorite, I remembered.

"Hmmm. I don't know."

"Green chilies, beans and tortillas?"

"Ask Lance."

Still, all during those teen-rearing times full of baking, cooking, calories and carbohydrate loading, I saw the miracle of the loaves and fish in our home on a daily basis as God provided despite my son's gigantic appetites.

God always provides. Have faith. Someday, the children will grow up, leaving a large cash bonus where the food budget once was. In the meantime, thank God each day for the blessings of the loaves and fishes in your home!

What basic need can you turn over to God today?

Further study: John 6:5-14

Day 3

When Do I Get the Spa Treatment?

Every good and perfect gift is from above, coming down from the Father of the heavenly lights, who does not change like shifting shadows. James 1:17

In our house, there are two kinds of towels: the velvety guest towels and the ragtag collection of everyday "carwash" towels. The carwash towels are easily spotted by the frayed edges, rips, grease spots, and bleached patches from someone who secretly dyed his hair behind locked doors. Their delicate see-through condition makes them one-of-a-kind. Most are a cross between a paint rag and a dishcloth. These noble towels have lived through two wars, two teenaged boys and all their friends, four cars, and fifteen pets. Now, mostly I take the carwash towels to the gym to dry off—as if a rag the size of two dinner napkins does very much.

The velvety guest towels have hung in the bathroom nearly untouched by human hands since my sons left home to be on their own. They match, are always neatly folded on the racks, and color-coordinated to the rest of the bathroom. When do they get used? I guess when I have overnight guests. But I'm not a guest, so I never consider using them.

While doing some repairs on the usual bath, I had to use the guest bathroom. After I showered, I reached out for a carwash towel. The cupboard was empty! The only thing left to dry myself off with were tissues or the hallowed guest towels.

I trembled as I reached out to touch one, expecting lightning to strike. I thought I heard the command, "Thou shalt not…." But no! That was my idea, not God's. The towels are soft. They are thick. They feel like fleece. They'd never been treated with disrespect by being wadded up and left on the floor to ferment.

It felt wonderful to dry off with them. It was a real vacation experience!

Thoughts took me from work and home to a spa resort! I had not left my own bath, but was experiencing luxury.

God gives us great gifts. He expects us to use them! His blessings are not to save to use "someday." Use and enjoy them now. When you think of God's good gifts, think of the lesson of the bath towels. You're worth it. God loves you, and he's proving it.

What great gifts has God given you?

Further study: Ezekiel 34:26-31

Day 4

The Christmas Surprise

Go, walk through the length and the breadth of the land, for I am giving it to you. Genesis 13:17

When I went looking to buy a family home, the sales people showed me some one-of-a-kind features.

"What's this?" I asked when a realtor showed me inside something that could only be loosely categorized as a single-family residence.

"The bathroom."

"You're kidding. It looks like an RV toilet in a closet."

"Whatever."

"And what's that smell?" I wanted to know.

"The slaughter house. But today it's windy. Most days, you won't smell it."

Single moms are not often known for fat financial portfolios. The sales people and mortgage bankers had laughed at me many times and said the same thing, "This is all you can afford. You don't have enough income or a big enough down payment." So instead of what I asked and prayed for, most showed me shacks.

Not Mary. She was just starting as a sales professional and really listened. I had been dreaming of a home for my family for twelve years. Mary zeroed in on what I needed.

"It has to be a three-bedroom house in a decent and safe neighborhood."

"Right-O! I can do that!" she promised cheerfully.

If God and Mary are on our side, who can be against us?

"Here's one!" she pointed at the computer screen. "But it's financed under a government program. Let's see if you qualify. Yes! As a 'moderate income' family!"

That was the nicest compliment she could give me on a teacher's salary.

"All the names on the contracts go into a hat, and then they draw a name."

Later when she called to tell me about the drawing, she said my name was not the first drawn. My heart was on the ground, thinking this was another demolished dream.

But Mary somehow still sounded hopeful. When she called again, she explained, "Often, buyers in these programs don't pass a credit check. Number One name didn't pass. You're Number Two. They want to check your credit."

A speeding snail sprints faster than government paperwork moves.

A month later, the boys and I gathered around the lit Christmas tree. It was our tradition to lie under it and look up through the fragrant evergreen branches. One at a time, we shared our wishes. The boys talked about theirs.

"Mom, what about you?"

I sighed. "Well, if it's God's will, may we have that house of our own."

The day after Christmas, Mary called me with the answer, "The house is yours if you want it!" It was our best Christmas surprise ever!

Not long after, we all three walked the length and breadth of the land that showcased our family home. To others, the yard looked like dirt. To us, it looked like possibilities. The twins and their twelve bicycles now had room to breathe.

God delights to give you your heart's desire, but it will be in his time. Keep thanking him, praying and believing!

What thanks can you give to give to him today?

Further study: 1 Thessalonians 5:16

Day 5

The Angel Who Wore a Hard Hat

For he is our God and we are the people of his pasture, the flock under his care. Psalm 95:7

Who can you call on the emergency hotline? Being out of range of the auto club for help and a long way from home is a good way to find out. Does God take care of his fleet as well as his flock?

It was only two days from getting back to home in Arizona, and the four of us were eager to start this traveling day early: my thirteen-year-old nephew, Chris, five-year-old twins, and me, the mom. We were finishing a month long road and camping trip.

Once my teen nephew plopped down in the passenger seat and my five-year-old twins got settled in the back seat, the car slanted like a skateboard ramp. The passenger side tire was as flat as a fly swatter.

Living in an isolated area where dirt roads and rocks gave me flats as often as people get their hair trimmed, I was joyful. Three thousand miles, we'd been through rain, hail, carsickness, burned foil dinners, smelly sleeping bags, bears, welts, scrapes, and visits from the Tooth Fairy to the campgrounds as the twins kept losing teeth. Now all we had was a flat tire!

"Hey, guys! Big deal! We'll be out of here in less than ten minutes. Who wants to time us?"

Chris flexed his muscles, happy to be chosen as the man on this trip, unscrewed and wheeled the spare around to the front, and started on the lug nuts. They didn't budge. The adult-sized teen grunted, groaned and nearly dislocated a shoulder putting his muscle into loosening the nuts. Nothing moved. Then he put his feet into the effort.

"Uhh. Aunt Jo. Look!" Chris said. He stood on the wrench, and it bowed like a curtain rod. The nuts were on so tight I wondered who had welded them.

"What could be wrong?" I thought.

The National Park campground where we'd spent the night was empty except for gnats and mosquitoes. We'd all run out of clean clothes and fresh fruit from farmers' markets. Once overweight, the weekly envelopes of trip money were looking downright skinny.

A few weeks before our road trip, I had taken the car in for complete service including rotating the tires. I chose the routes, and packed the camping gear, clothes, and food. *The tires?* How had the mechanic put the tires back on? Why, with an air wrench, of course! That handy tool saves mechanics hours and knuckles, and it was now the cause of our trouble.

I prayed, "God, you are the master mechanic, and the best auto club a woman could have. Help us! We can't do this on our own, and we don't want to spend the rest of the summer in this beautiful park."

"RRRRRRRRaattatat! RRRRRRR!" The sound was coming from the campground restrooms. A utility truck now parked in front of the building.

Chris went inside the men's room. There he found a construction worker, Charlie, repairing the building.

Soon, the two of them walked toward us, Charlie in a scuffed yellow hard hat and safety goggles. I was stunned when I saw what he carried in his hand: an air wrench.

Charlie was an angel in a hard hat sent to our rescue. He and Chris changed the tire faster than my record and we were on our way.

At the nearest town, I learned the tire didn't need repair. It only needed air.

"No charge, Ma'am," the mechanic said. "There's no hole, just a loose valve stem. Have a good trip home!"

God had proved to us that we are not just the flock, but "The fleet under his care."

How has God handled a desperate need in your life?

Further study: Acts 16:22-34

Day 6

The Super Sled

Moreover, when God gives any man wealth and possessions, and enables him to enjoy them, to accept his lot and be happy in his work—this is a gift of God. Ecclesiastes 5:20

"SNOW!" Cheryl cried aloud in her bedroom as soon as she looked out the window! The girl was surprised seeing the trees holding the white powder on their branches! In all of her seven years in the town, she had never seen snow that piled up in a thick fleece blanket and sparkled in the sun. It topped the red mesas and flowed down the sides like glaze on a cake.

She rushed into her mom's room and shook her awake. "Snow, Mom! Lots of it! Come see!" Mom snapped on the radio to find out school was closed for the day for the first time in this town. She would have a day off work, too.

Mom made a fire, dressed her young son and daughter for the cold and sent them to the yard to experience snow.

Hours later, she called "Come in now, children!"

"We're not tired yet, Mom! Can we go to the hills, please?" Cheryl pleaded. "We could sled!"

Before Mom backed out of the driveway, she thought about a sled. The stores were closed. Cardboard? The trash man just came. Was there an old board lying around in the yard? Nope. Old paneling? None of that either.

The small girl poked into a kitchen cupboard. She asked, "Mom, will this do?"

Soon Mom, holding Ernie on her lap shrieked with joy and slid on the icy slope. Then Cheryl. Then Mom and her little one.

Of all the sledders on the hill, theirs was the most unique of all. No one else had a COOKIE SHEET!

Giggling and laughing as it picked up speed and dumped them near the bottom, the three played together all afternoon in the novelty of snow. Mom noticed the late afternoon shadows stretched purple across the snow as the sun changed to red. She brought her children inside. This wonderful bonus day was full of blessings and joy.

"We have to wash this up," Mom said, holding up the battered cookie sheet.

Now with bent edges, dents and deep scratches, it would never be the same again.

Mom and Cheryl washed the cookie sheet, and then gave it to Ernie to dry. They tucked it back into the cupboard.

Investing time with your family and children creates moments to hold on to forever. How will you seize the moment today?

Further study: Psalm 92:1-5

Day 7

Never say "Never"!

"For I know the plans I have for you," declares the L*ORD*, *"plans to prosper you and not to harm you, plans to give you hope and a future.* Jeremiah 29:11.

When I handed over the money and the bike race entry form to a smiling mom, she handed me Lance's race number and asked me, "Are you racing today, too?" Are you kidding? Eight miles on a bicycle? But I just politely replied, "No, not today. I would *never race bicycles*."

Guess what I learned from that? Saying "never" sets off an alarm in Heaven. Suddenly the background music stops and God leans forward, fully at attention. He smiles and says, "Oh, really?"

To me, bike racing sounded about as fun as bathing the cat. I looked down at my thighs that were as thick as hams and a bulging waist. I just figured that it came with the territory of motherhood and middle age. Soon, I would need to buy clothes another two sizes bigger.

Instead, just months later, I spent the worst Christmas ever in the heart unit of the hospital. My heart symptoms were stress-related. I was now in danger of metabolic syndrome. The message was clear: change my lifestyle or die.

First, I had to stop matching portions with my sons and going to bed early because I had had a bad day. It had not been a good way of handling stress. Exercise would be a better alternative. However, there was no gym in our community at the time and I chalked up treadmills to be as boring as filing papers. But there were always a dozen or so bikes at our house.

So I humbly asked bike racer Lance to help me get started. He was not enthusiastic. I was slow and it was hard work peddling because those teeny bike seats are like sitting on a tablespoon when your rear is as wide as a picnic table. He hooted with laughter as I wobbled down the road—until I crashed into the back of his bike. Not on purpose! Honest!

Over time, I got better and began losing inches as well as pounds. I found an exercise partner. Several days a week, we did an aerobic workout together.

The summer the boys moved out on their own, I found myself standing at the entry table as a fit, firm, and much slimmer version of my former self handing over the money and forms for a bike race. It wasn't eight miles on flat land. It was twenty on rolling hills.

The ride was challenging pedaling with a headwind, but I ended the race joyfully. I had come a long way from thinking exercise was as fun as bathing the cat. And God had known it all along.

What can you do today to take better care of yourself?

Further study: 1 Corinthians 6:19-20

Questions

Count Your Blessings, Even When the Toilet is Overflowing!

How will you create new ways in words and actions for counting your blessings?

What positive thoughts or verse can you focus on to change your attitude through all situations?

How are you blessed today?

Reflections:

____

____

____

____

____

____

____

The best way to keep children home is to
make the home atmosphere pleasant
and let the air out of the tires.

Dorothy Parker

Week 5

There's Always Room For Improvement! It's the Biggest Room in the House!

Day 1

When in Canada, Bring Your Teapot!

> *"Which of these three do you think was a neighbor to the man who fell into the hands of robbers?" The expert in the law replied, "The one who had mercy on him." Jesus told him, "Go and do likewise."*
>
> Luke 10:36-37

As Arizonans thousands of miles from home, we didn't know what to do about rain. No raincoats ever hung in our closets. An umbrella was something we might use in a school play. Windshield wipers in southern Arizona died of sunstroke, not overuse. Until this rainy afternoon, our desert tents and gear had not had a moisture test.

In the last four days as I drove east across Canada, rain had enveloped the compact station wagon with the four of us inside, the five-year-old twins, my teen nephew, Chris, and me. Even when I turned into a spacious wooded campsite, the three boys glumly glanced at everything misty with rain.

"Cheer up, Boys! This rain can't last too much longer!" I quipped, remembering our summer monsoon rains that lasted about an hour, and then shut off like a faucet. After a monsoon, the Arizona ground would soon be as dry as crackers.

To make shade and a rain cover, most campers string a waterproof tarp between trees. Not me. I still clung to the monsoon theory. Though we were being assaulted by rain, Chris and I spread out the large dining canopy over the pine needles under some evergreens.

Soon the tarp was collecting puddles while I coaxed a hot dinner from the sputtering camp stove. With the crunch, crunch of footsteps in the gravel, I turned toward the joyful Canadian voice, "So you're all the way from Arizona, aye?" The senior's raincoat was nearly dry. I nodded. "Haven't seen another car around here from Arizona for a month or more." I noticed his puzzled look when he spied the three damp boys huddled on the tarp. The rain dripped over them and their dinner.

"Doesn't rain much in Arizona, I hear."

"Nope," I told him. "We've never seen it rain this much before ever!"

The smiling senior offered, "If it stops raining, I'll come over and start a fire for you." He jaunted back to his dry, warm travel trailer in which he and his wife were able to watch our camping drama. It was better than TV!

Chris and I set up the two-person tent camper for him and one twin. That's when the zipper died on the tent trailer. I threw a tarp over the tent door. Chris and one twin started a board game inside, but drops of water squeezed through the keyhole and wet the board. An explosion of cards blasted out of the tent. Chris announced, "That's it! I'm finding a dry place!" Chris had to be desperate as he sprinted to an outhouse nearby. Pit toilets were at the top of his hate list. Soon his face was pressed against the screen as he sucked great gulps of clean air and the smell of freshly washed evergreens. He was dry, but not a happy camper.

My Canadian campmate returned in his black rain gear carrying a hot pot of tea. "It's not dry enough to make a fire, so I brought you something to warm you up," he said. His smile was cheerful. The ceramic pot of tea he held up belonged in a tidy kitchen, not so far from town. The shiny black surface was decorated with delicate flowers and gold trim. I thanked him and headed for the privy door. "Hey, Chris!" I coaxed, standing at the privy door. "Open up!" Chris squeaked open the door wide enough to see the elegant pot of hot tea. Soon we all sat in the car, enjoying the warm drink. Our sense of humor returned as we were filled with thankfulness. Out of the thousands of miles we traveled, we would remember that couple's act of kindness to strangers as an example of Jesus' command for us to go and do likewise for our neighbor.

Who is your neighbor?

Further study: Matthew 5:43-47

Day 2

The Fresh Herb Surprise

Therefore, as God's chosen people, holy and dearly loved, clothe yourselves with compassion, kindness, humility, gentleness and patience. Bear with each other and forgive whatever grievances you may have against one another. Forgive as the Lord forgave you. And over all these virtues put on love, which binds them together in perfect unity. Colossians 3:12-14

Volunteers Sherry and Ellen rushed into the community kitchen where they fed scores of needy people every weekday. Flushed with excitement, they each clasped a long sprig of a green leafy branch, and breathlessly offered them to the Master Chef, Jean.

"Look, Jean! My friend gave me this herb for the spaghetti sauce today. She said it's basil. I'm so excited! I've never cooked with fresh herbs before! Just those dry sprinkles of Italian seasoning. You can teach us!"

Jean took a leaf, studied it and told them, "To know what an herb is, you can rub its leaf in your fingers. The smell is very strong. That will help you to know what it is."

The chef took a sprig, rubbed its leaves between her fingers and smelled deeply.

Ellen asked, "It is basil, isn't it?"

Jean replied, "No, definitely not. It doesn't have a strong smell. The leaves aren't smooth and shiny."

"But this has wide leaves just like basil!"

"It does have wide leaves, Ellen." Jean smelled, "But no, it's not basil nor oregano, either. I don't think we can use this in the sauce today."

"Why not? What is it?" asked the chef's assistant.

She smelled the leaves a third time. "A weed!" pronounced Master Chef Jean.

They all laughed hard and hugged. "It's okay, ladies. We're all learning!"

How often do our riffs with others, unlike this one, end with hard feelings and wanting to get even? Do we rerun cruel words or actions, and keep getting mad all over again?

From *Man Bites Dog*, mystery author Ellery Queen wrote "… the two women exchanged the kind of glance women use when there is no knife handy."

The apostle Paul, who wrote this passage and about half of the New Testament, had plenty to be angry about. Once he became a believer in Jesus as Messiah, Paul had many trying to kill him. He was in three shipwrecks on the Mediterranean Sea, was stoned and beaten, was a prisoner dependent on his friends to feed him, and spent much time in a dark cell until he was killed as an enemy of the state.

Yet Paul followed Jesus' example modeled for us, forgiveness bound up with love. He forgave daily and thanked God for the opportunity to tell his guards about Jesus.

If you had or didn't have a loving home with parents who valued you, you now have a model of forgiveness and love. We are God's family. He never stops loving us, or forgiving us. Neither should we stop forgiving and loving.

Can you hand over one hurt to Jesus today? He can help you heal and forgive.

Further study: Colossians 1:10-14

Day 3

Have the Ghosts Left the Area Yet?

> *For as high as the heavens are above the earth, so great is his love for those who fear him; as far as the east is from the west, so far has he removed our transgressions from us.* Psalm 103:11-12

As I drove through the city for the first time in years, I peered closely at the neighborhoods, stores, and business district, looking for ghosts. Was it the season of black and orange? Nope. Was I there with a ghost hunter team searching for paranormal activity? Uh-uh. One of my fifty-six hobbies? Never. Researching? Not that, either. Still, I searched for shadowy figures around a familiar restaurant, run-down apartment and the downtown area.

"Whoever am I looking for?" I wondered.

In my mind, I got the answer immediately. Perhaps I had expected to spot a twenty-something woman with hair that had never been altered at a beauty salon; someone who said "yes" when they should have said "no." That girl was me! I was not going to find her here, but I had been holding onto shame and memories of the past, failing to forgive myself.

Just as cities rebuild and lives renew, so it is with us when God forgives us. After all, just as the city had an entirely new skin, so did I. Every one of our body cells generates new cells over the years. I had been made new! God had forgiven my past sins, and so must I!

When it comes to relationships, we create a major wedge by not forgiving, especially when it comes to ours with God. It is necessary to forgive ourselves and move on.

What will it take for you to give your mistakes to God today?

Further study: Matthew 5:23-24

Day 4

R-E-S-P-E-C-T Spells "Respect"!

Rise in the presence of the aged, show respect for the elderly and revere your God. I am the LORD.

Leviticus 19:32

She was just like a tiny Navajo grandma from *Arizona Highways*. Against wind-buffeted red cliffs, she had walked tall among her sheep, her wrinkled face like an apple doll. The grandma, dressed in sensible moccasins, a tiered skirt to her ankles, and velvet shirt, was wearing her turquoise. It had been fashioned by the silversmiths in the family.

As the double-cab pick up parked next to me at the bank, Grandma was tucked in the back seat, sitting as straight and tall as if she were twenty again. However, she looked to be close to one hundred years old. As the young man and woman wearing jeans and casual shirts stepped out of the truck, the woman with long loose dark hair reached in the truck bed and expertly flipped out a step and a cane, positioning them to help Grandma. She had obviously done it many times. Then she offered her arm.

Grandma accepted it. Respect and family ties united the three of them as they walked together into the bank, helping each other as needed.

Her act was pure respect, plain and simple—just what God expects of us.

In a time when many are often the "sandwich generation," relieved to finally have peace and quiet in an empty nest, they soon after may be responsible for other aging family members. An attitude makes all the difference. The older generation can be a lot of trouble, consuming more time and money out of busy lives. Perhaps God is prompting us to be respectful and joyful to share time with all generations. We, too, will be in the Geritol Generation some day.

How can you show respect to someone today?

Further study: Exodus 20:12

Day 5

Who is Calling, Please?

The idols of the nations are silver and gold, made by the hands of men. They have mouths, but cannot speak, eyes, but they cannot see; they have ears, but cannot hear, nor is there breath in their mouths. Those who make them will be like them, and so will all who trust in them. Psalm 135:15-18

Paula had been sound asleep when the phone rang so late, she thought it might be a family emergency or about Uncle Harry, who was going downhill fast. "Huh?" she answered sleepily. "Hel-lo." The recorded voice began, "I'm Ra-chel of Card Services. I'm calling to tell you your spec-ial of-fer of a 6.5 in-ter-est rate is about to expire." Paula slammed down the phone.

On her way to work, Paula noticed the car was running on an eyedropper of gas, so she stopped to fuel up. As soon as she picked up the nozzle, the gas pump broke out in a female voice, "I'm so glad to *see you!* You're just the person I wanted to talk to!"

The voice told her she was hungry for popcorn, a soda or candy bar available inside the station store. Right! It was 5:15 in the morning! "No talking gas pumps, please!" Paula found a well-used "mute" button and pushed it.

When she got home after a crazy work day, Paula took a deep breath, enjoyed a hot cup of tea, and then played back her messages. The first through seventh: "Hel-lo! This is an important message for Priscilla. If this is Priscilla, press one. If Priscilla cannot come to the phone, press two." No Priscilla at this number. Number eight call: "Hel-lo. This is an im-por-tant mes-sage about a state-sponsored Adopt-a-Wolf Program. If you want to save a life and have your very own wolf at your doorstep, and share the ex-per-i-ence of a lifetime, please press two now!"

Number nine: "Hel-lo. We are calling to confirm Priscilla's order number DK309867-5 for two elephants and a month's supply of large animal food. You are one of the first fifty to order, so included is a free bonus African acacia tree so your new pets will feel welcome!" Paula had ordered no such thing!

Later, when she wanted to withdraw money to buy gifts, Paula heard, "Enter your three-digit identification number. Pick from the following options 1) access accounts, 2) check balance, 3) trade account balances with someone else." She was so stunned trying to process this information, she didn't press anything. The message kept going.

"That is not your number. Good-bye!" None of these offered a customer service option where she could talk to a real person to stop these calls. How Paula missed the personal touch!

Naturally, I have exaggerated this story. While our current lifestyle becomes dominated with push-button and recorded transactions, online bill-paying, and robotic customer service representatives, God's open door policy has not changed since the beginning. Relationships with him are personal. That's the bottom line. They involve sticking one's neck out, being concerned and genuinely interested. God does that with each person forever and always.

How can you improve your relationship with God today?

Further study: 1 John 3:1

Day 6

Does God Know You?

[Jesus said] "Not everyone who says to me, 'Lord, Lord' will enter the kingdom of heaven, but only he who does the will of my Father who is in heaven. Many will say to me on that day, 'Lord, Lord, did we not prophesy in your name, and in your name drive out demons and perform many miracles? Then I will tell them plainly, 'I never knew you. Away from me, you evildoers!'" Matthew 7:21-23

From the far north country where he lived, Rick called his Grandma thousands of miles away to ask, "What was my father's middle name?" As this twenty-one-year-old had no father in his life except the first month of his life, Grandma was curious.

"Rick, why do you need to know?"

Rick told of that day how a stocky, dark-headed man came into the outdoor recreational store where he worked.

The man wanted to buy a canoe, he said, "… to do a little fishing in Arizona." That was where Rick was born. His hazel eyes matched Rick's as well as the curly hair, but it was when the man signed the warranty card on the canoe that Rick's eyes opened wide with surprise. He felt a chill. Their last names were the same, and stranger still, the handwriting was the same as his own. He peered at the man. The man looked back at him idly noticing Rick's name tag.

Grandma told Rick the full name. It was an exact match.

But Rick's biological father, who had just packed the canoe in his truck and driven off, was father in name only. He had not seen Rick or his brother since the infants were a few months old when he legally severed his parental rights. He was no real father.

Building a relationship takes time. Contact and an open heart for others is modeled for us by God. We reach out to others for the love of it. But how close do we feel to people who only contact us when they want something or have a crisis?

Phone calls, remembering birthdays, giving encouragement, e-mails, and shared time keeps us close. Just a card to say you're thinking of someone keeps the doors of friendship open.

Do we give God the same time to build a relationship as with our families and friends?

God is a loving friend who invites us to keep close all of our lives. How do you start building a relationship with God? You don't need a stamp or a computer. He's a thought away 24/7. Just talk to Him and keep reading and learning about Him through his words in the Bible.

How has God been there for you every day?

Further study: Proverbs 3:3-4

Day 7

Love Looks Like a Black and Green Pie

Love is patient, love is kind. It does not envy, it does not boast, it is not proud. It is not rude, it is not self-seeking, it is not easily angered, it keeps no record of wrongs. 1 Corinthians 13:4-5

Aunt Marie modeled unconditional love. While caring for an invalid husband full- time, she would make time to do something for anyone else who had a need, too. It wasn't easy.

One July day in the Southwest, the temperature was somewhere between chili-roasting and a brush fire. Aunt Marie wiped her wet face with a paper towel and told me,

"You bring the twins and your mom and come for dinner tonight about six. I am planning to make stew and a lemon pie, your favorite."

As she stirred the thick pie filling in a double boiler, Marie noticed she was out of yellow food color for the lemon filling. I offered to go to the store. "No," she insisted, "I'll have to make do."

The heat had done her in, I could tell. Normally, she would get exactly the right ingredients, even if she had to hike across the continent for it. Marie reasoned she would make the coloring from the other bottles. The filling was now the color of the Caribbean, a luscious blue-green!

"Marie!" Frank hollered from his recliner. "I want something to eat!"

The back of his bald head showed above the chair like a boiled egg in an egg cup.

She held a perfect bacon, lettuce and tomato sandwich in front of him on a plate. "I don't want it now," he snarled. "I'm going to bed."

That's the way it was a dozen times a day. Bed to recliner. Recliner to bed. Never a thank you or an apology.

No matter what life threw at her, Marie smiled. Not today. She poured herself a large glass of cold tea, and then slammed the empty glass on the counter with the words, "That Frank!" It was the closest she ever came to complaining.

"But the meringue will be perfect!" she said as she layered and twirled the peaks of white meringue, then popped the pie in the oven for a five-minute browning touch.

"Marie!" Frank hollered as he shuffled to his recliner with his few strands of hair askew. "I want some ice tea!"

Before she could finish the pie and check Frank, the meringue looked like a torched marshmallow!

At dinner, Mom commented, "Marie, you've outdone yourself with this delicious meal." Marie smiled humbly and looked at her plate. At last, she brought out the pie—the only one she ever made that hadn't been perfect. "Sorry about this," Marie started, "but...." It was delicious!

Love went all around the table that night in smiles and thanks from *everyone*.

It was the first time I ever heard Frank say, "Thank you, Marie, for the dinner."

Sometimes others know just how to push your buttons to make you angry. Using the love passage as your guide, what can you do differently to smooth things out with love?

Further study: Ephesians 4:2-5

Questions

There's Always Room For Improvement! It's the Biggest Room in the House!

How have you encouraged someone this week?

Initiate a call or letter to someone you want to touch today.

How would you develop a plan to keep in close touch with someone important to you?

Reflections:

You can always tell a real friend.
When you've made a fool of yourself,
she doesn't feel you've done a permanent job.

Week 6

Doing Time for God Does a Body Good!

Day 1

Got Time?

But the fruit of the Spirit is love, joy, peace, ***patience,*** *kindness, goodness, faithfulness, gentleness and self-control.* Galatians 5:22

Tiny Irene Maxwell stood in comfortable stacked heels at the door to her prison classroom at the County Jail. Soon she would meet the three prisoners who wanted reading lessons.

No one had been successful before, but the men had told their supervisors they wanted to read.

The officer walked the three muscled men with their hands clasped behind them to the door. "If you need anything, Mrs. Maxwell, I'm right here at the door," the officer assured her.

Shaved, bald, and decorated with tattoos up to their thick necks, the prisoners marched in, sizing up their teacher. Their arms bulged with muscles so rounded that they couldn't bring them down to their sides.

"Sit!" They did. Then the tiny teacher spelled out the rules. "If you really want to read, you're going to do everything exactly as I say. I will have you reading, but it will be my way *and* it will take time." The wrestler-sized men looked down at the tiny grandma.

She wore a look as hard as any prisoner they had ever met. They glanced at each other. They could have snapped her in half, but they had worked for the privilege of learning to read.

Then, one prisoner hung his head and admitted, “We got time.”

When Irene told them what she wanted them to do first, one prisoner spat, “What! That’s stupid. I’m not doing that!” Immediately, the men on both sides of the table shot him a look. So did Mrs. Maxwell as she leaned forward and stared into his eyes.

Each of the men had his hands in the air, drawing down each letter of a simple word and sound. It was the beginning.

With God, living relationships such as growing and learning begin with the fruits of the spirit, including patience. Give yourself time! God isn’t finished working on you!

What relationships in your life need more of your time and patience?

Further study: Hebrews 12:1-2

Day 2

Is Our God Big Enough To Trust With Lost Keys?

I lift up my eyes to the hills—where does my help come from? My help comes from the Lord, the Maker of heaven and earth. Psalm 121:1

Somewhere in the midst of the chaos of packing to move on a tight deadline, I had lost track of the keys to the rented moving van. It seemed like a bigger problem because we lived so far from town.

I made a long-distance call to the rental truck company. "I picked up this moving van yesterday and now I can't find the keys," I told the voice at the other end.

"Where are you?" I looked out over the tiny group of houses and miles of spacious skies in this isolated post where I had taught school for a half-dozen years. "One hundred miles away."

"Oh. And where is the nearest rental truck dealer?"

"About thirty miles away. So can my mom pick up some extra keys from your office and bring them here?" I suggested hopefully.

"We don't have any extra keys."

Soon after, a white sport utility vehicle stopped inside the fenced school yard and parked. Longtime friends Bill and his wife Mary stepped out. "We couldn't let you leave without saying goodbye," Mary said with a hug.

Without another word, Bill surveyed the packing in the truck. "Whoa, boys, stop!" Bill said quietly, looking over my sweating crew of children thirteen and under. "Let me help." Bill restacked and tied off the load in sections the way it needed to be for safe travel. Mary helped me pack inside, but as the hours passed, we found no moving van keys. Within twenty hours, I had to leave the teacher housing spotless. As soon as the three of us reached our new destination, we were to report as summer camp volunteers.

I told Bill about the key crisis. "You're a logical person," he told me. I nearly gagged on that remark, thinking I am about as logical as a plate of spaghetti. "The keys are here somewhere and you'll think of where. Have patience!"

"We have got to go now. But let me have your summer address," Mary said.

"Sure," I answered and began checking my purse for a card with our summer address and phone. Unfamiliar keys gleamed. A warm flash of relief flooded over me! I retrieved the moving van keys, which had hidden inside my purse through all the activity and packing.

There are times in life when something seems so impossible we may feel that help is just as unlikely, but God provides all the help we need, and on his time line, too!

Compare some recent situations. How would you rate yourself in waiting for God to handle your needs?

Further study: Psalm 130:5

Day 3
Bread from Heaven

Wait for the LORD; be strong and take heart and wait for the LORD. Psalm 27:14

It was baking day for the "Basket and Bag Ladies," and I was up before sunup to start fresh bread for the community visitation program. I had only a narrow window of time to make the yeast bread to drop off at the church, still fragrant and warm, before I rushed to work.

Rain pelted on the windows like a shower of gravel. It can be touchy to get perfect loaves at our high elevation, especially during stormy weather. "Oh, Lord," I prayed, "let this bread be blessed for those who receive it today, that it is the perfect texture, great taste, and most unpredictable of all, rises perfectly. It can only happen with your help! Amen."

I looked at the warm liquid and yeast sprinkled over it that would make the bread into a perfect mushroom shape or collapse like a flat tire. Instead of frothy foam, there were only a few bubbles like pimples on a pre-teen. Not a good sign! When I shaped the bread and pushed it into the warm oven, it felt like eight cans of dog food instead of eight small loves of multigrain bread. It took little imagination to visualize eight teeth-breaking loaves emerging from the oven ready to decorate the yard like river rocks!

I decided to whip up some apple strudel muffins, just in case, and not having all the ingredients, I got very creative. I became so involved that I did not notice that God had, indeed, blessed the bread. All had beautiful round tops. Before I had given God the chance to prove himself, I had whipped up something else.

The strudel muffins proved to be a culinary mistake. But the bread, why it was a gift from Heaven!

Waiting on the Lord is an important concept. His time frame is different than ours, but he always responds.

If you ask the Lord for help, do you wait for it, or charge ahead?

Further study: Micah 7:7

Day 4

A Peaceful Heart

"Peace I leave with you; my peace I give you. I do not give to you as the world gives. Do not let your hearts be troubled and do not be afraid." John 14:27

"I'm sure you'll find our ship docked behind this hotel with the other river cruise ships. I'll just wait here while you look!" my cousin Vivian had said. In the muted morning light coming through a wall of glass of the luxury European hotel lobby, the vigorous eighty-year-old found a comfortable lounge chair, pulled her legs up, adjusted the pillows, and arranged her colorful packages and luggage around her.

As she looked around the lobby that was as big as a new car showroom, Vivian was beginning to feel the effects of jet lag from her flight. While guests worked intently on computers in the business center, they were lulled with soft music, muted décor, custom flower arrangements and sculptures. So was Vivian.

From one end of the dock to the other behind the hotel, Vivian's friend Manny and I walked, searching each bow for the name of the one booked for a week-long cruise. I was feeling frantic, being the only one of the three of us who had never traveled abroad.

When I verified with the desk clerk the ship was somewhere near the hotel, I told her with urgency, "We have to board in the next hour."

"I'm sure you'll find it," Vivian waved. "I'll just wait here."

So Manny and I walked again toward the dock, this time from a different direction. He pointed, "Look! That's your ship!"

When I returned to the lobby, there was a commotion near Vivian in the lounge chair. Surrounded by her packages, Vivian had fluttered off to sleep. She had looked like a bag lady! Worried about the hotel's reputation for timely service and over the top accommodations, a doorman was shaking her awake. "Sorry, Ma'am, you can't sleep here!"

Vivian internalized peace in napping in the lobby. Jesus, too, promises us his peace from worry and troubles, even when jet lag slows us down.

How would you rate yourself as having a calm and peaceful attitude in all circumstances?

Further study: Psalm 119:165

Day 5
Tattletale Talk

You will keep in perfect peace him whose mind is steadfast, because he trusts in you. Isaiah 26:3

With detailed reports, organization, and packing up the kindergarten classroom for the summer, Miss Roberts was feeling overwhelmed. It had been a terrible tattle-tale day. Miss Roberts wondered what had happened with her children who normally got along so well. Maybe they were cranky as they spotted the public swimming pool now open on weekends. Was it something hot and windy in the air so close to summer? Perhaps everyone was as eager as she was for a summer change of pace.

She took a deep breath as six-year-old Andy approached her. Andy tiptoed to Miss Roberts, and in a stage whisper began, "You know what…." Then Miss Roberts asked, "Andy, you aren't a tattletale, are you?"

"Just a little bit," he admitted.

Coming from a place of peace makes a big impact on others. It is a strategy for diverting anger. The quoted passage is a reminder that we are to be steadfast, firm, and determined. We know God is in charge of the earth, our own world, and our lives. We can trust him for the outcome of any problem. That is the key to perfect peacc.

Compare when you feel at peace the most and the least.

Further study: Matthew 5:9

Day 6

Just Trucking Along

There is a time for everything, and a season for every activity under heaven. Ecclesiastes 3:1

The handsome young man trotted eagerly towards the truck showroom with his request. A foot shorter than his customer, the salesman immediately sized him up as well as the dented four-wheel drive sports utility vehicle he had just stepped out of from the passenger side. It was time for new wheels, the salesman decided, not to mention bumpers, antenna, a working air conditioner, and other niceties. The salesman was already lost in thought figuring trade-in value when the youth approached him.

"Hi, I'm Travis Russell, and I would like the brochure on the newest Toyota Four-Runner."

"Sure," the salesman led him to a rack. Travis flipped through the brochure, and then rattled off a number of technical questions about engine size, power, and towing capacity. The salesman was surprised. The customer had researched his product and knew what he needed.

"So, instead of just talking about it, why don't we take one of the new ones out for a spin?" He held out the keys and pointed to a silver model parked outside the showroom.

"Uh, I would love to, but I'm only fourteen."

"Ooooo-kay," the salesman countered, spinning the keys around on his finger. "Come back when you're older!"

There is a time for everything. It is easy to worry, push, think, calculate and predict, but all such things are a waste of energy. There is a perfect time and a perfect solution for every problem. God determines the perfect time and answer.

What have you been wrestling that with God will solve be solved in his time?

Further study: Isaiah 40:31

Day 7
A Time for Everything

The L*ORD* *is my shepherd, I shall not be in want. He makes me lie down in green pastures, he leads me beside quiet waters, he restores my soul.*

Psalm 23:1-3

Days working and raising a family had flowed into each other until the only thing I recognized was Saturday afternoon to rest. Whoever wrote Ann Landers and told her school teachers only work six hours a day and have three months off should be stapled to a hall bulletin board for a month!

Recognizing teachers needed to spend more time at home working on internet research and lessons, our school district offered refurbished computers for sale that any teacher could afford. I bought one.

Keith, the technician, warned me, "It's slow." I didn't ask the obvious question, "How slow?" I soon found out. Between our rural internet provider and the computer itself, I now had time to make a tossed salad and grilled cheese sandwich while I waited for it to connect.

Though I was grateful for technology at home, I grumbled to my mom. Aware of my long hours, commute, and schedule, she quipped, "Just the thing you need!

Otherwise, you may never get a chance to eat!" I hadn't thought of that.

In our world, multi-tasking and working with impossible lists of tasks with even fewer people than ever is more common than paperclips. Stress and illness go together when there is no time for good food, fun or rest. God knows it. That's why he kicked back after creating the world, just enjoying the day.

How can you build in time for rest and fun this week?

Further study: Genesis 1:1-2:2

Questions

Doing Time for God Does a Body Good!

How do you prioritize your time with God and your family compared to a job or responsibilities?

How would you balance your time for investing more time in what matters most?

Reflections:

Why not go out on a limb?
Isn't that where the fruit is?

Frank Scully

Week 7

"A" is for Action!

Day 1

Smacked into Realty with a Rubber Band

But I gave them this command: Obey me, and I will be your God and you will be my people. Walk in all the ways I command you, that it may go well with you.

Jeremiah 7:23

A fat orange rubber band with a knot in one end, a tool for physical therapy, hung on my doorknob and made me feel so guilty, I thought about hiding it away. "It clashes with the bathroom décor anyway!" I said to myself. A few weeks before, my doctor showed me three simple exercises to help strengthen the shoulder I had injured falling on ice during the winter. Now that I was no longer lifting and sliding boxes that were nearly my own body weight at work, and had a long vacation ahead, the shoulder could heal completely.

The young doctor explained, "Just lifting weights and doing a circling motion with weights is not giving you the resistance you need to heal that shoulder." So standing behind me, the doctor monitored and corrected me doing the exercises, in which I caught the band in the door and pulled the rubber. "Start with eight reps, then work up to three sets of fifteen." Why, that would be easier than running the vacuum! Every weight-bearing exercise I had been doing at the gym was with fifteen to twenty reps.

Besides, I was coming up on a long vacation. The first day through the seventh, I did the exercise with the rubber band faithfully. It was a cinch! On the eighth, I was headed to the gym and would work on the shoulder there. On the ninth, I was swimming, so the shoulder got a workout. Pretty soon, the rubber strip hanging on the doorknob had become a dusty reminder of my broken promise to me and the doctor who had coached me so thoroughly. I felt guilty. Like the Israelites, I was turning away from the right path. It had taken me a week to turn my back on the fat orange rubber band and the simple exercises to heal me. Then I remembered that the reason the injured shoulder had been so slow to heal was my *disobedience,* specifically not following directions.

I have always been stunned to read how often the Israelites—God's chosen people—had turned their back on him. Even those who had witnessed his parting the Red Sea for them to cross on dry land did not remember for long. God gave them food and water in the desert in places where a divining rod could not locate the liquid in the arid sand. Their creator had kept them safe camping around scorpions and poisonous critters. Once they moved in and got downright comfortable in the Promised Land, it was "Hello Canaan!" and "What lovely Canaanite women!" and then, "Goodbye God! Thanks a million! We will be okay from now on."

So, no more excuses. I got out the tool and did my reps easily. You know what? It took five minutes.

How would you rate your obedience to God? What area of your life needs more of your commitment?

Further study: Hebrews 4:12-13

Day 2

Getting Over the Impossible

Jesus replied, "What is impossible with men is possible with God." Luke 18:27

"I'm Jo and I'm a slob." I could imagine standing up in a 12-step meeting and admitting this. Before God stepped in, I figured I could never overcome this habit. Not so.

Do most women have an immaculate home and never battle disorder, dirt, and chaos? One mother's children learned to give themselves a bath, make their beds and fix their own meals by the time they were four. She never had any of them show up in a dripping mud-covered trash bag after being towed on an inner tube behind someone's four-wheel drive.

"Dear Lord, please guide me and help me overcome my sloppiness." Not long after, I forgot I'd asked Him. If you pray for rain, then get out your umbrella. If you pray for God to heal you of sloppy habits, then stock up on rags. I didn't.

One day, the doorbell rang and I answered wearing my project clothes covered with a layer of drywall dust, which I'd tracked through the house. My hair stuck out of leg holes of the underwear on my head. On the porch were two women staring at me with their mouths open: Miss County Beauty Winner and her sponsor. They were just on time for their appointment for coaching on the pageant speech. Miss Beauty's immaculate hair sparkled with a tiara. Her heels and designer dress were stunning. The appointment was in my day planner, but I hadn't looked at it that day. Grand Mal Embarrassment set in.

God has a sense of humor, you know that?

As a teacher, I added to my income by painting houses during the summer.

I went to the first house to work. There was dog poop welded to the rug in the corner. I cleaned it up. Dust bunnies there were big enough to knit together into a Volkswagen. To say there was disorder in that house was like calling a boat wake the same as a tidal wave.

After that fifteen-hour day, I went home, vacuumed, cleaned toilets and washed dishes. "I can actually do this," I realized.

The next house had an office and a kitchen that needed painting. Before I started the kitchen, I gathered up stinky used baby diapers littered along the wall. The cupboards moved, not because of a poltergeist, but because of ants: millions of them.

I went home to disinfect and organize my own cupboards.

"Very funny, God!" I told Him. "What's next?"

The next three houses were about the same, and I changed for the better. Having an uncluttered house helps to have an uncluttered life.

Organization is constant, *not a one-time process.* All of us can organize most of the trouble spots at home and life in five-minute segments. Over time, none of it will be cluttered.

God indeed did the impossible with me as he can with you, and with a sense of humor at that. I have, at last, come to terms with how much organization is necessary for a smoother life with fewer dirty dishes and more time for adventure.

What impossible habit can you give to God today?

Further study: Exodus 3 and 4

Day 3

Why Is That Fly Following Me?

The night is nearly over; the day is almost here. So let us put aside the deeds of darkness and put on the armor of light. Romans 13:12

If anyone sweated on the sidewalk one hot school day, the drops sizzled into steam right away. Even the ants stopped moving while the scorching sun was out. The classroom cooler was not much help. It worked better to fold notebook paper into fans and use them to cool off. So I propped open the classroom door in hopes it would relieve us of the symptoms of heat stroke.

When Jordan sprinted into my classroom for the last reading group of the day, he pulled the door shut behind him, banging it hard. Then he wiped his face. "Whew!" he whistled with relief. "That fly has been following me around all day." After a pause Jordan added, "What does he want anyway?"

When God is talking with us, what does he want anyway? He wants our attention, worship, offerings and love. Putting him first is like the wise advice given to caretakers. Take care of yourself first or you won't be around to take care of someone else. Part of our job as multi-tasking women is caretaking and modeling, whether it is for children, teens, or older adults. That starts with our kneeling at the feet of God every day in prayer and Bible study. We can go into our worlds and shine with his light.

How much time do you set aside for prayer and study? What difference has time with God made in your life?

Further study: James 4:7-10

Day 4

Carved in Granite? My Life?

[Jesus said] ..."And surely I am with you always, to the very end of the age." Matthew 28:20

I pulled into the grocery store parking lot and was stunned with surprise. I felt faint, then angry. Where is the justice system when you need it?

Someone's fat car was straddling *my parking place*, the one that had been mine for years! There wasn't even enough room between it and the next vehicle to land a paper airplane!

Should I call my auto club to tow the trespasser away? Should I ask God to strike it with lightning?

Then I got hit with the bolt of lighting instead. Just what made this *my* parking place anyway? Was there a parking curb with my name on it? Was there a recessed brass plate in the asphalt honoring me for my generous support of this food store through two sons, six cats, three dogs, two floods, three vehicles and seven sets of tires? Well, no. It is, after all, a public place. That day, I had to find another parking space and think about what it means to break away from life on auto pilot.

How often do we go on autopilot expecting that life will always be the same? It isn't, and God does that to us for the excitement and to force us to be flexible. Scary, isn't it? Life continuously changes. It's assuring that you can lean on God through all the changes. He's certainly going to throw new experiences and surprises at us.

The legendary David slew the giant Goliath when he was a youth, maybe fourteen years old. He didn't become king until twenty-six years later when he was forty. In the meantime, Jerusalem's King Saul threw spears at him, chased him down to kill him while David lived in caves and hid out with Saul's enemies, the Philistines. David and his men were homeless and often hungry. Don't you think David asked God, "When? When will I be king? You promised!" David's life was full of surprises. So are our lives.

I had plans. God had plans. His won out. I retired early from teaching because of health issues. When I had it planned down to the payday for retiring from my second career, God stepped in with surprises and jolted me out of autopilot. I retired earlier. Later, I realized how much God's timing was better.

The next time you're stunned to find out you've been living on auto pilot and God changes your life, smile and be glad! God is busting you out on manual mode for your own good!

What part of your life is on autopilot? How will you change that?

Further study: Esther 2:5-23

Day 5

No is a Two-Letter Word

"My son, do not make light of the Lord's discipline and do not lose heart when he rebukes you, because the Lord disciplines those he loves, and he punishes everyone he accepts as a son." Hebrews 12:5-6.

When he was a baby, he couldn't stand being alone at night. My Gordon cuddled up face-to-face with me until I could feel his soft breath on my cheek. It haunted me. I know researchers consider it bad for a child to sleep in his mom's bed, so I planned to move him when he was bigger.

As he grew, he liked to watch me write at the computer. I fixed a playpen for him next to me. He made happy sounds at first, and liked his naps there. Later, he was bored and wanted to be all over the office. One day, I found he'd chewed the computer "mouse" wire through. When he pounded on the keyboard, he was busted. "No! This is Mom's writing place, not yours! No!" I'd put him back in his playpen. Just as God does with us to keep us from harm, I enforced boundaries.

Because wild critters up to the size of a small bear sometimes made themselves at home in my yard, I held Gordon tight when we went out to sit and rock in the porch swing.

One day, before I started to install a new deadbolt lock on the back door, I checked Gordon to find him taking his afternoon nap. I would have to keep the door open while I worked on the lock. But his round toddler belly was rising and falling with each breath. So I began replacing the deadbolt, working slowly. Only five minutes later, Gordon stood at the closed glass door that adjoined the room, making all kinds of noise. Now the great outdoors was calling to him, and I was blocking his door to fun.

"Just wait, Gordon! I'll take you outside." Later, my tomcat Flash Gordon walked unsteadily out in the yard. For his own safety, he was not alone.

Just as we may do with God, my cat continually tests his boundaries. Have you noticed that God doesn't give us everything we want? He loves us as well as disciplines us, even as adults. We don't always get the job we want, or may not live exactly where we planned. Our goals may need to be modified because our chosen direction is not the best or is foolish. Perhaps we later learn we were protected from hardships or harm. As parents do with children and owners do with pets, God's directions, discipline and guidance are in our best interests. Are you accepting God's discipline in your journey?

Further study: Job 38:8-11

Day 6

Does My Spiritual House Need Painting?

[Jesus said] "Why do you look at the speck of sawdust in your brother's eye and pay no attention to the plank in your own eye?... You hypocrite, first take the plank out of your own eye, and then you will see clearly to remove the speck from your brothers eye."

Matthew 7:3

From his outfit of many colors, I guessed that the tanned older man who rang my doorbell liked to paint. He stood at the door with a smile. I'd never met him before, but already we had something in common. I like to paint, too.

"I'm Ralph, and I've been painting houses in this neighborhood for twenty years."

Hmmm. He could certainly start on up the four neighbors' houses that were faded, peeling or unpainted altogether. I told him so and rattled off names, addresses, and serial numbers.

"I can paint your house and do very good work," he offered.

"What!" I thought. "My house!" I felt miffed! Every year, I touched up my own house. Nearly every summer while I worked as a teacher, I painted houses to supplement my income. Did he really think *my* house needed painting?

"Thanks, anyway, but I do my own painting!"

Once he left, I went outside and looked high on the edges of the house with new eyes. There was so much peeling paint and bare wood on the trim boards I'd never finished, it looked like nachos. How did I overlook that? While I'd been thinking of my neighbors' peeling houses, I'd failed to notice my own. That summer, I planned to launch a block improvement program to help my neighbors repair and paint their homes. But first, I had to start with myself and my home. It did need painting, not just touch-up, but the whole thing. I got out the ladder, tools, and started scraping.

My spiritual life at times is like my house that needed painting. What good does it do to have the Bible on the table do if I don't take time to study? While I commute, the prayer list is tucked into the dashboard for prayer. Am I praying? One Bible study is tucked in a briefcase; another in a bag. Are all these just props to look good or are they tools that I use for growing and learning?

Without action, any tool is useless. The real deal is jump in and do it! You'll grow and learn!

How are you using your spiritual tools today?

Further study: Hebrews 12:1-2

Day 7

And God Commandeth, "No Dyslexia Allowed."

Being confident of this, that he who began a good work in you will carry it on to completion until the day of Christ Jesus. Philippians 1:6

Before the soothing sound of indoor waterfalls became popular, I had one inside the walls of my first home. It was easier to ignore than to investigate it and utter aloud a four-letter word that was forbidden in our house.

At a business meeting, one of the top saleswomen in my store told our boss, "We can sell. We just can't do the math!"

That was the word: M-A-T-H! She'd be my soul-mate forever. So someone else had trouble with numbers? "Amen!" I breathed to myself.

But God wouldn't let me stay where I was with number problems. As an adult, I learned that I have trouble with numbers in the same way that some readers have with dyslexia. They see letters in reverse and black shapes dancing on the page like a chorus line. But like readers with disabilities, someone struggling with a learning problem can learn tricks and skills to move forward.

A guest using the bathroom at my first house asked, "Where is the water running? I can hear it in the wall."

"Some people have built in vacuum systems. I have built-in sound effects! They came with the house. After all, there are no puddles, no mud, and no leak!"

A few weeks later, part of the street collapsed, forming a cave-in large enough to garage four motorcycles and a small pick-up. A few days later, the canyon was oozing a new creek over the pavement. That's when the city employees noticed and turned off the water.

"Mrs. Russell, the broken pipe is under your house."

"But it's concrete!"

"Yes, and the pipe is broken right in the cement. Your insurance company will decide what to do. But they won't pay for the water. You'll have to pay for what you used."

"I didn't use the water! It was running down the street!" I protested.

At the water department, Lorraine rattled off a formula as common to her as a phone number. "Don't worry; it's only blah blah per gallon. With it leaking that many gallons, it will be the price per gallon times how many. You can do the math."

Forced into figuring it out myself, I used the city's formula and gasped! The water running down the street had enough digits to buy a luxury home on the golf course!

"Linda, please pray for me!" I was choked with tears as I confessed my problem at church. "The water bill for the broken pipe is more than the price of my house! I don't know how I can handle this!"

Thinking logically, Linda asked, "How did you come up with that amount?"

"It's what the city uses as a formula."

She looked at me strangely. No wonder. Working with the financial office of the school district, Linda was used to dealing with water bills for the entire area schools, six in all. She was in on the planning and groundwork of the newest school that cost in the high six-figures. "Sure," she said, "we'll pray for you. Please let me know how it comes out."

When the bill came, I learned my four extra zeros were more powers to the ten than I needed! God had to be chuckling up there.

God loves us all so much he gives us problems in our weak areas. Trusting him to work on us makes us stronger!

What weak area is God working on in you?

Further study: Romans 8:26-27

Questions

"A" is for Action!

List what you do to support your spiritual life.

What areas of weakness need work?

How do you involve your family in spiritual growth?

Reflections:

Life is what happens
while you're making other plans.

Robert Balzer

Week 8

Another Day, Another "Ooops"!

Day 1

Holy Smoke, the Church is On Fire!

"For the LORD your God goes with you; he will never leave you nor forsake you." Deuteronomy 31:6

An ancient mobile home with floor tiles curled like tortilla chips was the Mercedes of the places where we met for worship services in the rural church district. The metal building set on the bare desert floor had electrical wiring that was manufactured just after Thomas Edison made his invention public. When the days were 110 degrees outside, the trailer rocked with the squeaky floor fan.

Pastor Jim cranked up his voice to be heard. "We are celebrating 'The Lord's Supper' today, and we will have that after classes this morning."

I pulled the accordion door shut for my group of four. Our children's class sang the action song, "Father Abraham had many sons, many sons had father Abraham, I am one of them and so are you, so let's all praise the Lord! Right arm! Left arm! Right foot! Left foot! Chin up!" Though our faces ran with sweat and our hair was sticky with dried salt, I smelled something that was not sweat, nor incense to hide the bathroom odor.

"Look!" my student Jack pointed to the wall, "There's smoke coming out of there!" It was the electric box! The church was on fire!

Retired fire marshal Joe exploded from his chair, giving orders as he ran. "Turn off all the power! Bring me the hose!" Several men kicked in the wall and helped to stop flames that could have destroyed the entire building in ten minutes.

Pastor Jim exclaimed, "Whew! Lucky you were here, Joe!" Handshakes, smiles and back-slapping followed.

With all the excitement focused on getting the fire out, the children in my class lounged against a table and realized how thirsty they were. Without electricity, the fan was silent and the building hotter. "We can really praise the Lord that everyone is safe, especially these wonderful children here!" Pastor Jim pulled Crystal close. She dropped her head and wiped her mouth with her sleeve. It was then that the adults realized that all of my class had purple moustaches. The "Lord's Supper" would have to wait!

God is with us through all the fires of our lives—and the grape juice. Even beyond the "Amen" of our prayers, God is still there, watching for our needs.

How is God with you today?

Further study: Psalm 118:6-7

Day 2
The Magnetic Designer Coat

All men will hate you because of me, but he who stands firm to the end will be saved. Matthew 10:22

The black wool designer coat arrived in a slippery plastic bag. As I pulled it free, I saw and admired its tailored feminine lines, faux fur collar and cuffs. The women's dress coat was a perfect fit! Most of the time, I had been forced to buy outdoor coats from the men's section of a catalog because of arms and body as long as a railroad car.

When I put the new coat in its place next to other dress clothes, I noticed it had a magnetic quality that could only be matched by the pencil-sized magnets vets feed to cows so unwanted tidbits do not stay in their stomachs. Still, I loved the coat, despite the lint, metal filings, hair, fur, dust bunnies, straw, grass cuttings, and any carrot peelings within a mile that stuck to it. When returning home after wearing it, I checked over my shoulder to see if the chirping birds following a treasure trove of nest materials stopped at the door.

One day before a memorial service, admiring the coat's styling and class, I vigorously brushed the garment until it was as deep and dark as velvet.

When the service was about to begin in the quiet chapel, I quickly found a seat next to someone I knew. "How are you?" I asked her. She didn't answer the question, instead remarked, "You need to use a lint brush on that coat."

"I did, actually. This designer coat has rare magnetic qualities. I still love it, though."

As a meticulous person who sparkled in her job because of her attention to detail, she hated it, so much so that she turned away and cried to several friends, "Hey, there's Sally all by herself! Come on, Julie! Let's go sit with her!" The two of them moved to sit on the other side of the aisle away from the offensive lint-catcher. I sat alone, still loving my designer coat.

Though later she apologized, she taught me the reaction to my designer coat is the way some people feel when you mention God or Jesus. They just cannot move away fast enough. Nevertheless, we still love him!

How do you show the world that God has taken over your heart?

Further study: Galatians 2:20

Day 3

Oh, For the Love of Green Beans!

Above all, my brothers, do not swear, not by heaven or by earth or by anything else. James 5:12

As I struggled to move a box that was as large as a refrigerator and twenty-five pounds heavier than I weigh, one strap broke and the cardboard bottom came loose. Only a few more inches and the boxed bathroom vanity wobbling on the small wooden platform would fall two stories to the floor and break to pieces. My customers in the large retail store were waiting below. Both man and wife had arms crossed and tapped their toes impatiently.

On the high lift truck I used for retrieving boxes, I wore a safety harness so I would not fall or be injured. I stopped to think and regroup. "Gee, this is not age-appropriate! Not only am I a woman, but a senior. The ideal candidate for this job would be someone who can leap tall buildings in a single bound with a toilet under each arm, a vanity between their knees, and a thick pad of sold orders clutched between their teeth!"

"It will be just a minute!" I called out sweetly to my customers. I pushed and shoved the box, but it changed shape as it moved, stubbornly resisting me. It teetered over the edge, and I quickly slid it forward, nearly running out of platform to stand on.

"Oh, s---!" I cried. High above the racks and displays, close to the metal rafters, I heard the sound travel and echo, not just in my department, but over four others.

With one word, I had changed my Christian witness. Years before, I had lived in an environment where swear words were as common as salt. God's name was the paprika in fancier exclamations. I had picked the swearing habit up, too, but had also broken it. Now @#!%! God forgives, but the word could not be re-called.

How can your conversations with others reflect Christ in your life?

Further study: Titus 2:1; Exodus 20:7

Day 4
Child Collateral?

For I am convinced that neither death nor life, neither angels nor demons, neither the present or the future, nor any powers, neither height nor depth, nor anything else in all creation, will be able to separate us from the love of God that is in Christ Jesus our Lord.

Romans 8:38-39

Sherry, the insurance representative at the hospital, glared at me from her desk with a stern frown as she clutched one of my diaper clad twins. Her small office had suddenly burst at the seams with babies, their gear, and a twin stroller the size of a small car. The baby boy who cooed into her face expected a smile from her. Only a few weeks old, he knew he was the catalyst for love, smiles, and hugs. Not with her! The unhappy grown-up shuffled papers on her desk and began spelling out terms.

"I see that you still owe after your primary insurance carrier paid most of the bill for the twins and their intensive medical nursery care. The second carrier will not pay because you signed up too late. There is a considerable balance left. I see that you and your husband owe quite a bit on other bills too. How do you plan to pay this? What will you use for collateral?"

She swiveled in her chair toward me, holding the baby tighter. Though I thought the hospital's delivery and care of the babies would be considered *services,* Sherry considered the babies *goods,* and she had a tight hold on one just to prove it!

The fact was, I had no idea how I would pay an amount equal to three years' salary. Before I spotted a blue padded cell where the one twin would stay as collateral, I swept the child out of her arms, gathered my gear, and told her, "I don't have any answers right now. I will get back to you."

Fortunately, though I thought Sherry and I were the only adults in that tiny office, I had later learned a fiercely devoted father had been sitting in on that conference at the hospital. God! I arrived at work a few weeks later and found my desk wallpapered with checks for nearly the entire balance of the bill. All checks were from the second insurance carrier.

God showed his love then as he does always. He sits in on all our challenging conferences, and his son, Jesus, has already served as collateral on our debts. There is nothing more needed. He has it handled.

What can you ask him to handle for you today?

Further study: Psalm 116:1

Day 5

May I Take Your Order Please?

The body is a unit, though it is made up of many parts; and though all its parts are many, they form one body. So it is with Christ. For we were all baptized by one Spirit into one body. 1 Corinthians 12:12

At the end of the first day of school, Mrs. Park walked her new first grade students to the bus loading area. She kept the wiggling mass in order as she stayed to monitor the children in lines to make sure they got on the right bus. Still curved around her neck was the newest tool the district offered—a microphone for a child in her class who was hearing-impaired.

Jenny, another teacher's student, had not seen such a tool, so she stared at the curved black shape around Mrs. Park's neck. Then as the teacher walked by, the girl tugged on Mrs. Park's blouse. She had to know, "Do you work for McDonald's?"

Everyone has something special that sets them apart from others. We might focus on a physical limitation as blight, but the Lord does not. He has *chosen* each of us!

Have you considered that as the Lord knit you together wonderfully, he gave you a combination of abilities, skills, and perhaps afflictions that make you one of a kind?

Each one of us contributes as one of a sum of parts, as part of a team. God does not see our afflictions, but zeros in on the wonderful whole of us.

Based on God's love and affection for you, what merits more of your attention—your gifts or your afflictions?

Further study: 1 Corinthians 14:14-31

Day 6

Where Can I Resign From the World?

The earth is the LORD*'s, and everything in it, the world, and all who live in it.* Psalm 24:1

My son, Travis, decided he wasn't wanted when he was a teen. Never mind that the blessed event happened over fifteen years before when I had been married. He was not part of a planned pregnancy. In the old days, when technology was in the testing stage, I didn't even know I was having twins until three weeks before their birth. Surprise!

I told him often, "Travis, you're our free bonus gift! I love you so much!"

As a teenager, he was questioning everything and figuring out who he was. The quieter of the twins, he was often overshadowed by his outrageous brother. I called the school counselor right away, praying and remembering that Travis belongs to God first. She spoke teenager, chauffeured him to the nearest fast food place and bought him ice cream. That helped.

Travis still had doubts about his family loving him. He announced he was running away to Grandma's summer home. No matter that she wasn't home for the winter and the heat was off. It was the coldest month of the year. There was electricity, phone and water. Packing up his largest pack, outdoor magazines, and a compacted case of dehydrated food, Travis headed out, not looking back. It was a short hike, and he wore new boots he had worked for and had bought himself.

He didn't answer the phone when I called Grandma's. The first day, I checked on him. He'd opened up the sofa bed and was stretched out on it wearing sweaters, a jacket, plus two pairs of thick wool socks. Travis was reading his outdoor magazines: each grouped by title. His large pack was leaning against the bed. He showed no signs of moving back home. With Grandma's stash of canned goods, my son had enough food for months.

"Hi, Travis!" I greeted him cheerfully.

"Hi," he said glumly, not looking up from his magazine.

I talked with him awhile until I got tired of one-syllable answers, plus "I guess" and "Who cares?"

"Are you ready to come home? Your brother and I miss you!"

"So?"

You can guess he wasn't ready.

Each day I checked on him. Then one day, I came over and mentioned, "Grandma wants to talk with you. You know the phone is working."

I dialed the number and handed him the phone. All I heard on this end of the conversation were one syllable answers, "I guess," grunts, and "Okay." After he hung up, Travis packed up his things to come home, ready to rejoin a family who loves him.

He came home a man with a purpose, with honor and self-respect. Travis went on that year to win a school-wide short story writing contest. His essay on honoring parents was published in the newspaper. He earned a letter in track and won "Who's Who in American High Schools."

God wasn't finished with him then and isn't now. He has plans for him and for you, too.

If ever we fight the feeling we don't belong, we can remember God's love is always there! He made us one-of-a-kind with special gifts. You belong to God's family, no matter where you fit in the world!

How has God led you on your journey so far?

Further study: Proverbs 3:5-6; Jeremiah 1:6-10

Day 7

Brenda's Little Brown Hen

But Ruth replied, "Don't urge me to leave you or to turn back from you. Where you go I will go, and where you stay, I will stay. Your people will be my people and your God my God." Ruth 1:16-17

"Get your brown feathered butt out of here!" the widow Brenda hollered at the chicken in her living room. "I got company coming today. I don't want none of your pet dander in here where folks are going to be sitting!" The barrel-shaped senior tossed an empty Skoal can toward the sofa. It was a show. She fiercely loved her feathered pet.

What looked like a garden-variety scruffy brown hen ran out the door, but not for long. It was like symbiosis, a science arrangement between two different animals. They needed each other. Brenda needed the eggs and the company; the chicken needed Brenda to provide a safe haven from prowling coyotes. Every night, the coyotes left signs all around her aging rounded mobile home; they cased the place. But Brenda proved she was a good shot.

Her company came, crowding around a table the size of a cutting board, and then Brenda saw the chicken perched on the bulging stuffing on the sofa arm. "What are you doing in here, you plucky thing? Shoo! Out!" Brenda ordered.

Though her words were harsh, Brenda's heart showed through. The feathered pet ambled around the porch, and then poked its head in. Soon the hen was back on the cool sofa perch. Brenda stared hard at the brown hen and bellowed, "Get out of here before I make you into chicken and dumplings!" It made a quick figure eight in the hot sand outside, and then was cackling from the sofa.

Brenda cut its cackle short with, “Get out of here before I make you into fried chicken!” Another lap and she threatened “chicken tacos;” then “chicken noodle soup;” then “creamed chicken on toast.” The hen always returned to its perch as if it were family. It was.

No one else on the surrounding ranches thought of Brenda’s chicken as anything more than what it was a source of eggs. Just as Brenda would not abandon her hen and Ruth would not leave Naomi, we are to cling to God with the same loyalty and tenacity. He will not let us be separated from him. With God, we have a name, a family, and a destination.

How do you fit into God’s family today?

Further study: Revelations 3:5

Questions

Another Day, Another "Ooops!"

Name particular things in your life that tend to separate you from God.

Make a list of all the ways God has shown his love for you.

Reflections:

The best time to repent of a blunder
is just before the blunder is made.

Josh Billings

Week 9

Looking for Love in the Right Places

Day 1

Looking for Love

Dear friends, let us love one another, for love comes from God. 1 John 4:7

On a dark morning that any retired person might consider obscenely early, Jean opened the back door to let her pet outside for a short time into the fenced yard. In the snap of a finger, the furry creature was out of sight. After a reasonable amount of time, Jean flipped on the floodlights and blasted the yard with light. Still no cat. As she stepped down in tattered pink furry bathroom slippers and raggedy pajamas, Jean shuffled along and checked each of the cat's favorite hide outs. No cat.

When the previous neighbor family had moved, they had simply left the tabby and white cat behind with no food and no plans. The pet had detected Jean's soft heart with the first meal she missed, climbed the fence, and mewed her way into Jean's heart and home. It was easy. Now the pet was an important part of her family.

"Love! Love!" she cried, a little louder each time. Soon the neighbors on each side could hear her cries. "Where are you, Love?"

A little embarrassed, Jean thought, "Now everyone knows. I'm a crazy old woman looking for love in all the wrong places!"

The world thinks it knows us by what we drive, but truly the world knows us by how we love. When we know God, we show love.

What does showing love look like in your life?

Further study: 1 John 4:17-21

Day 2

Just Follow the Smell to the Suitcase

"Then neither do I condemn you," Jesus declared. "Go now and leave your life of sin." John 8:11

There was no doubt that five days of sweaty activities shared with his brother, friends and family was a real outdoor experience for Carl. Hiking, exploring, biking, kayaking, in-line skating, boating, fishing—there was hardly time left for Carl to dress for his part as best man at his brother's wedding.

Even though the island temperatures were misty and cool, all that activity resulted in stinky clothes that did not make it to the hotel laundry. Every moment he could enjoy before the wedding with his soon-to-be-married brother, Carl did. Now it was time for Carl to repack his duffle bags and suitcase. Three days of travel were ahead: an overnight ferry trip to the mainland and two days on the highway before getting back to his cabin. The young man was jamming wadded up dirty clothes on top of the folded clean ones in his suitcase. His dirty clothes would smell up the whole suitcase.

"Do you want a bag for the dirty ones?" his mom offered. "That way, all you have to do is pull out the bag and wash those clothes."

"No," Carl replied. "I can tell the dirty clothes just by the smell."

Sin is the same way. The odor permeates and affects everything else in our life. Once we know what God considers right and wrong, we need to act on it and make changes. Sometimes, it means cutting time with friends involved in activities that are wrong for us or our families. In his goodness, God has chosen us. We need to choose him by choosing good.

What deliberate change do you need to make in your thoughts, actions, or activities?

Further study: Matthew 12:30; Exodus 34:12-14

Day 3

Keep it Simple, Smart Girl!

Jesus answered, "The work of God is this: to believe in the one he has sent." John 6:29

Something was leaving deposits the size of a meatloaf in my yard every early dark morning about three. Then the thing got diarrhea. Yuck!

I searched the shelves of a large home project store for some kind of repellent that would keep this unknown trespassing night visitor off the lawn. Two containers smiled at me side by side. One had a label completely filled with long words. I had translated "urinate" to "pee." The other long words escaped my memory bank. Why should it take a college graduate degree and a dictionary to figure out what a product is supposed to do? There was no picture, either. No wonder the can was covered with dust!

The cheerful product next to it showed a picture running down the side of the label of all the critters it stunk out of the yard: dogs, cats, raccoons, skunks, squirrels, horses, goats, and somebody's pet pig. That was perfect for my neighborhood! On the front, it said simply, "Repels these critters from the area" and listed them. On the back, I read you could use this in a seed spreader or sprinkle it on. Simple? Why, yes! I bought that product, and it worked!

The product I bought is like the simple message that God gives us: He loves us completely and without limits.

How are you doing loving God and showing it in your daily life?

Further study: John 21:7-17

Day 4

Perfect Health!

"Young man, I say to you, get up!" The dead man sat up and began to talk..." Luke 7:14-15

As I drove my mother home from her forced medical incarceration in the local hospital, Jeane was joyful and delighted with simple pleasures. What a wonderful thing to be sleeping in her own bed again, to be in her own home, and to be welcomed home with dog kisses! Being home was a new lease on life and she was planning it out one activity at a time. She was on the phone all morning with friends chirping "Great!" and "Terrific!" while writing appointments on her calendar.

Though my friend, Connie, and I had planned an outing together, she was concerned whether Jeane could be on her own at home for a few hours. Now a doctor, Connie knew which of her colleagues had cared for Jeane and what her treatment had been. Much to Connie's surprise, Jeane herself answered the door. "Despite what you may have heard," she said as she opened the door, "I'm in perfect health!"

Connie responded, "So I guess the rumors of your death have been greatly exaggerated!

We all have been given a new lease on life when we accept Jesus as God, the Messiah, the one who completed his mission on earth by fulfilling prophesies hundreds of years before that he would pay the consequences of our sins and rise from the grave.

Any close brush with death due to illness, accident, risk sports, or injury can give us a sense that we have been saved and given another chance. Given time and a clean slate, what would you do differently in your life beginning today?

Further study: Luke 24:1-8

Day 5

The Valentine's Day Hype

An unmarried woman or virgin is concerned about the Lord's affairs: Her aim is to be devoted to the Lord in body and spirit. 1 Corinthians 7:34

When Valentine's Day comes, I often feel a pang of longing to be kissed by someone, to feel a warm body curled around my legs, and to be showered with dark chocolates from Brussels. Who doesn't when you're over twenty-nine and still good looking?

It does happen, but not in the form I was expecting. Lady Star puckers up and kisses me with enthusiasm, especially if, on her clock, it's time to get up. One cat curls her luxurious fur coat around my feet. The chocolates? You'd have to say this is a do-it-yourself project with cream, butter, cocoa, sugar, and time.

One time, I remember feeling relieved when a truck pulling in the driveway wasn't an electrician, plumber, or carpenter. It was a florist's delivery van. "Must be in the wrong driveway," I thought and waved him away. But he didn't go. Instead, he came to the door carrying a vase of flowers exploding in my favorite color: purple. The one-time gift surprised me. My children from Alaska had ordered them for me for this special day of love.

Paul mentioned that single people are valuable in the ministry. Singles can often be the odd one out during events geared for couples.

At my Sunday class, someone popped their head in to ask the widows, divorcees, and singles, "Anyone want to go to the Valentine's Banquet put on by the men this year?" With a vengeance that would go with a question like, "Does anyone want to go sky-diving?" three responded, "NO!" But after the door closed, Vera had an idea. It only took a few minutes for the Faithful Friends Class to plan a Valentine's activity that included everyone, and which allowed someone who needed a visit to have the party brought to her. It was a win-win situation!

What can you do to remember a single woman on Happy Hearts Day?

Further study: John 13:3-17

Day 6

Welcome to Miss Smith's Classroom!

You who seek God, may your hearts live!

Psalm 69:32

As the first grade teacher got ready for the new school year, Miss Smith felt as if she knew every student coming into her class the next day. She studied their test scores, read the comments from their kindergarten teacher, and thought about them as she decorated her classroom in bright colors. She set out a fish cut-out on each desk with each student's name and which bus they rode home or if they walked.

After nearly three months off school, her cherubs would rush happily into her classroom. Would they remember what they learned in kindergarten? "Please God, I hope so!" she prayed.

The next day was the first day of school! As she brought her students in and welcomed them, she showed them where to sit. Miss Smith took Rachel by the hand and led her to her desk.

"Miss Smith," Rachel asked, looking into her teacher's eyes a little frightened and bewildered, "did I go to school last year?"

No matter how many times teachers begin with students' summer amnesia, God gives us even more new starts than that. He loves us! If you have accepted God, will you recommit your heart to him today?

Further study: 1 John 3:16; Isaiah 57:14-16

Day 7
Lost and Found

Seek the L*ORD* *while he may be found; call on him while he is near.* Isaiah 55:6

Once a friend told me, "You're so right-brained, it should be against the law!"

The right-brain is the artistic and language side, while the left-brain focuses on numbers, facts, and organization.

For the last hour and a half, I had been driving Danelle around in search of a ranch house where she would pick up a puppy her sister had bought. I was steaming as I asked, "Do you have an address?" I asked, knowing it wasn't unusual for a country home to have nothing but a post office box.

"No."

"A phone number?" Not that either. "How about more specific directions?" I asked, getting more annoyed by the minute. I had headed east and west, tried every two track road with a county sign or none at all. Some had been two-track mud ribbons disappearing into the knee-high grass. "Why are you smiling?" I angrily asked her.

"This is my *lost and found time*!" She told me she was remembering the numerous times she had been lost during trips on home or foreign soil. While being lost often rattled me so much, I had nearly made myself sick, it did not upset her at all. She just planned more time into the trip. Now I knew for sure that Danelle, a gifted artist, was also so right-brained it should be against the law! "At this point, we're so lost, we might end up four states away," I told her. We both laughed. Both of us needed a Global Positioning System (G.P.S.) and a better grasp on time, planning and directions.

In church circles, the terms "lost" and "found" are used more than "red" and "blue" so that the words sometimes lose their meaning. The bottom line is, have you included the Lord in your heart, your life and your family? If yes, that's what "found" means. Adding God to your family brings a pillar of strength, love, and blessings like no other.

Further study: Revelations 3:20

Questions

Looking for Love in the Right Places

Just as a child needs a quiet place and time set aside for school work, we all need a quiet place and time to study the Bible. At a Christian writers' conference, one presenter had suggested ways to make a time and place for daily prayer and study. Emilie Barnes, author of *The Fifteen Minute Home and Family Organizer* as well as *The Organized Home Schooler* stated you need to start with a prayer area. It can be anywhere. In hers, she has a basket with the following in it: devotional, Bible, flowers, pens, note cards, prayer notebooks, and a prayer apron with handprints of grandkids on it. She sets aside a particular time each day to spend with God. This is a key for staying close to God.

Where do you pray and study or where would you like to at home?

____

____

____

____

What difference has it made in your day to start with God?

____

____

____

____

Reflections:

I have problems flown in daily
wherever I am.

Richard Lewis

Week 10

Where is Your Treasure Chest?

Day 1

In Case of Fire, Where is Your Treasure Chest?

> *"Do not store up for yourselves treasures on earth, where moth and rust destroy, and where thieves break in and steal. But store up for yourselves treasures in heaven, where moth and rust do not destroy, and where thieves do not break in and steal. For where your treasure is, there your heart will be also."*
>
> Matthew 6:19-21

Now that the danger was over, ten of us finished the Sunday school class talking about the terrifying message that had come over the radio during the recent wild fire.

Not even burned stumps were smoldering now.

"What did you set out to take?" was the question. We listened for each answer as we remembered the emergency radio alert: "Stand by! Stand by! All residents of the communities of… (they named them) be ready to evacuate your homes with one hour's notice."

It was no joke. The flames had formed 3,000 degree plumes that had incinerated homes and ranches, schools and businesses. The area had been tagged as a national emergency as the winds kept the fire out of control. Four communities totaling over 26,000 residents had been evacuated and left for shelters. News sources had predicted the wall of flame would hit the town sixteen miles away any time.

Miriam had been evacuated with her pets and she was staying with me under a gray ash cloud that left us coughing.

Now, the danger came to my town. My heart thumped so hard, I could feel it pulsating against my shirt. I had dashed into my home office to get the homeowner's policy, pictures, pet cages, food, and part of a collection. Miriam grabbed me by the arm. "Jo! There's time! There's time to get your stuff together!"

The wind switched direction, and at last, the fire was brought under control. Both our homes were safe.

Our conversation at Sunday school a week later was relaxed with the danger of the fire over. Our lists were similar. Then Dawn, remembering my sixty-seven hats, asked me, "So Jo, just how many hats did you have by the door?"

Sure enough, I had set aside a group of hats with the other items for the evacuation. Over time, I had found myself buying hats to soothe my wounded feelings, to help me through a bad week, to add a unique design, or to match an outfit. Why, years before, I had even lost one of my toddler twins in a large department store while holding one son's small hand and checking out hats! I had not even known the other boy was gone with the cart until Customer Service announced a Code Adam! They described my son.

Where your treasure is… Hmmm. Perhaps I think I had put too much emphasis on my hat collection. Think on the things that have top billing in your life and your home.

Where is God on your list?

Further study: Luke 12:15

Day 2

A Father's Blessing

"But love your neighbor as yourself."

Leviticus 19:18

The light filtered through the century-old stained glass onto family and friends crowding the historic church in Sitka, Alaska, for my son's wedding. In just a few minutes the ceremony would begin.

"If only Travis had a father to share the joy, prayers and blessing on his wedding day!" I thought.

A velvet curtain hid my son in the room next to the altar. Inside with him was his twin, Lance. They now both stood over six feet tall, handsome and well-groomed. In place of their usual outdoor sports clothes, the young men matched in tux coats with tails, satin vests, and trimmed collarless shirts. Also dressed in formal clothes, their friends' father Ben stepped inside with them. He and his wife, Jan, had traveled over 3,000 miles to be with them. When Ben walked behind the curtain, Travis's face broke out in a grin, and he hugged him as Travis became choked with emotion. Before this trip, they hadn't seen each other for three years.

Many in our small community where Travis grew up had helped with my parenting challenges, but our neighbors, Ben and Jan, had provided movies, frosted cookies, acceptance, and encouragement. They included Travis and Lance as "our boys" along with their own three sons.

Now, on my son's special day making this giant step and commitment to marry, Travis had asked Ben for a father's prayer and blessing. Loud sobs came from behind the curtain. I rushed forward and pulled it back. As Ben clasped my son's shoulder, Travis wiped his eyes with his hand, overcome with the emotion of this moment. "It's okay," Ben assured me. "It's okay," he smiled, squeezing Travis's shoulder.

Nothing is more honoring than a father's blessing. I had never before thought about Ben's dedication as a father, to his own children and mine, too. Ben had filled in the gaps where I, as a single mom, could not. He had taught them to be men.

Travis had just the right man to bless him and send him into his new world as a married man.

How can you show love and appreciation for your neighbors today?

Further study: James 2:8-10

Day 3

Corrine the Cool!

Refrain from anger and turn from wrath.

Psalm 37:8

Corrine figured with six, she knew all about children. She had nursed hers through teething, diarrhea, flu, homework, blood, boundaries, wounded feelings, reading and report cards. Now, though she trusted that her love for all of them was evident, she admitted that her most challenging, Nate, got most of her attention.

At the unlovely age of fifteen, Nate was giving her a hard time about reasonable family rules. His heated remarks were raising her temperature and blood pressure. She considered the idea of clobbering him with the biggest thing she could find—like the couch. Finally, he concluded, "But the biggest problem, Mom, is that you just aren't cool!"

That took her by surprise. Then she smiled and responded. "Nate, oh, yes I am!" Corrine searched the bookshelf for her high school yearbook. "And I'll prove it!"

She pointed to her best friend's note next to her own picture. Corrine's friend had penned, "Corrine, you are so cool! Love, Tracy." Mom and son exploded with laughter. It broke the tension. They could move forward in their relationship and continue to appreciate and respect one another—through the generation gap that had just been closed by two "cool" people!

What are some of the better ways you can divert anger?

Further study: Psalm 145:8-9

Day 4

I Was Blind, But Now I See!

But when the kindness and love of God our Savior appeared, he saved us, not because of righteous things we had done, but because of his mercy.

Titus 3:4

While in high school with a brand new driver's license in my purse, I was proudly driving my best friend home. I stopped at a stop sign, carefully looked, and then pulled out. Immediately after, I saw flashing red lights in the mirror and pulled over. Gosh, what had I done?

"How would you like to buy a new cop car?" the red-faced officer spat angrily. He rattled off a figure that was more than the mortgage on the family home. "Didn't you see the police car before you pulled in front of me?"

"Sorry! I thought I looked both ways. I didn't see you." I really had not seen him.

Soon after, I went to the eye doctor and found out that I am as near-sighted as a mole and have fuzzy vision so intense that it moved buildings and erased traffic signs. It should not have been a surprise I needed glasses, for in our family, you might have mistaken any of them for owls. Everyone wore—or was supposed to wear—glasses from china thin to telescope lens thick.

After the new glasses framed and changed my world, I again drove Connie home. I looked carefully for cop cars, not to mention buildings, dogs, and tumbleweeds. I screeched to a halt at each of the six stop signs between Connie's house and mine. Stunned to disbelief, I asked, "Connie, when did they put all those stop signs in?"

"Jo, the stop signs were always there!"

God's mercy protects us, and if we know him, we accept both him and a new way of seeing and living, just as I did when I first started wearing specs.

How are you using God's lenses in your life?

Further study: Romans: 11:29-32

Day 5

Visitors Welcome?

"Do not judge, or you will be judged. For in the same way you judge others, you will be judged, and with the measure you use, it will be measured to you."
Matthew 7:1-2

One day when the doorbell rang, Richard was at the front door and wanted to chat. I had always admired Richard for his organizational skills and clean house. His work area was spotless and his desk was ready for a photo shoot anytime. In fact, while he stood before me, he picked the lint off my sweater and pulled weeds. However, I did not invite him inside. Germs colonizing in corners, breakfast dishes in the sink, and the chaos of notes and magnets on the refrigerator might be offensive.

I returned to coordinating three complex activities and patted myself on the back for efficiency. Bed linens churned in the washing machine, cookies baked in the oven, and bread was rising on the counter. With a muddy trowel in one hand, and a timer in the other, I finished planting spring bulbs and came inside to check on the bread.

Later, the doorbell rang again and I groaned, thinking of our pastor's recent comment, "People don't like unexpected visitors unless it's the Schwan's Food man." This time, Jan was at the door, and I invited her right in. Why? Because her house usually looked just like mine, which could be categorized as "casual housekeeping."

I thought of how God warns us not to judge others. Had I judged Richard by not inviting him in or was I just afraid he would judge me? Who else in my life might I never know well because of judging?

Who can you welcome into your life today that you might have judged before?

Further study: Romans 14:10-13

Day 6

Just Vacationing Here!

But seek first his kingdom and his righteousness, and all these things will be given to you as well.

Matthew 6:33

With a change in the wind, the radio blasted an emergency order to evacuate five communities high in the mountains with the forest fire burning out of control. The command was sudden. Families as well as businesses and the branch college campus lost track of people. Not all the media got the message. A canned radio spot broadcasted the invitation for summer guests to come to a "pleasant resort community away from the heat and confusion," while 3,000 degree flames fanned forest and homes.

In a branch college campus twenty miles from the fire, a man decked out like a summer visitor stepped up to the library's check-out desk. He wore sandals, a wrinkled flowered shirt and shorts. Immediately the librarian's mouth opened with surprise and a smile. She recognized him as one of their dozen misplaced professors from the evacuated campus and greeted the man warmly. "John! We've been looking all over for you! What have you been doing?" John smiled. As John gestured to the gray sky and falling ash outside, he said, "I prefer to tell people that I'm *vacationing* here, instead of being an evacuee!"

When faced with challenges, do you know where you go to be found? To God, the source, the rock. No matter how unsteady and unpredictable life becomes, God does not change.

Give an example of a challenge in your life and the outcome.

Further study: Psalm 105:4; Hebrew 12:28

Day 7
All I Need Is…

"Again, I tell you that if two of you on earth agree about anything you ask for, it will be done for you by my Father in heaven. For where two or three come together in my name, there am I with them."
Matthew 18:19-20

Not long after a midnight call from Lance with the news he had recommitted his life to God, I picked up the phone on the first ring. It was in the middle of the day. "Mom, I need help." *Uh-oh.* With many parents, a child's next word is usually "money." But Lance and Travis knew better than to ask. What kind of help could I give from a distance?

It was February in Fairbanks. My sons had told me that often, in the extreme sub-zero temperatures, it was so cold that they could toss a cup of water in the air and it would come down as ice crystals. Lance pleaded, "I need prayer." He had told of the World War II relic heater in his rental cabin. In the dark early hours of morning, it had belched out black oily smoke and died. A repair man had told him it was not repairable. The landlord lived far away. At minus forty degrees, no heat is no joke.

For a week, Lance told me, he had been sleeping on people's sofas, "But there is much winter left. I can't just camp out on people's sofas for the rest of the winter. I need to be able to go back home."

Prayer. I could certainly pray. I called each of my prayer partners. We asked specifically that the Lord solve the problem of heat *in two days*. God answered sooner than that! Travis and his fiancé, Maria, guided another repair man to the freezing cabin.

While Maria drove Lance around in their truck to keep him warm, Travis stayed at the cabin until it was as toasty as Tahiti inside.

Sometimes we may consider prayer to be a last resort and think, "All I can do is pray." *ALL?* Prayer has even more power when praying with another!

God hears and answers prayer. Who can you partner with for prayer on a regular basis?

Further study: Matthew 21:21-22

Questions

Where is Your Treasure Chest?

Years ago, Pastor Jim's wife, Cathy, taught me how to write down prayer requests in a journal. This way, I had in black and white proof of God's answers. Sometimes, I would tally them up. Usually, it came out like this: sixty-seven answered "Yes!" Twenty- four answered "No" (and I would later know why) and seventeen without an answer yet. I would call that a "Wait."

Have you used a prayer journal in your life? If so, how has it been helpful?

____

____

____

____

____

What have you learned from prayers which were answered "No" or "Wait"?

____

____

____

____

____

Reflections:

The best way
to keep friendships from breaking
is not to drop them.

Week 11

Put Your Money Where Your Mouth Is

Day 1

Ask Josephine the Plumber!

> *Show me your faith without deeds, and I will show you my faith by what I do.* James 2:18

Put your money where you mouth is.

Talk is cheap. Prove it! All are catch phrases for moving from talk to action.

I looked down at the water pooled in the bottom of my very own bathroom sink that would not drain. "Lord, this happens to everyone else. *Why me?*" Of course, it had happened to me. It was a matter of time. My long locks had been shedding into the sink like a cat leaves furry evidence on whatever dark surface is forbidden.

"At least, it's a simple plumbing issue with three ways to fix it." I thought back on my work in recent years in the plumbing department of a large store. Not only did I know the black, white, green, galvanized, gas, and eggshell pipe, I could rattle off their many names and configurations as different as types of pasta. I taught, guided, demonstrated, found parts, cut and threaded pipe and advised many, all without ruining my necklaces and fancy scarves. Men had been surprised to be lead to "Joe" only to find out it was "Jo" instead.

How many tearful women did I coach through the messy business of fixing plumbing? Scores. With my help, my women customers knew how to replace a toilet, wax ring, water supply line, and shut off valves, and they knew they could do it! No longer were women stopped by not being able to get corroded things unscrewed. With sophisticated tools and my encouragement, female do-it-yourselfers had done things only some men attempted.

When I stopped for plumbing supplies at my store, I told my coworkers, "I'm going for the easy way," and I picked up a tool for pulling hair from the drain and a bottle of hair clog dissolver. At home before I poured the Jell-O-thick chemical in the drain, I paused to read the teeny print warning. It was a good thing I looked. It could ruin the finish. Oh. Forget that! I would have to take the pipes off underneath the sink.

It was time to put head knowledge to work and move on to heart knowledge. Even though I knew how from watching, from coworkers, and from diagrams how to rid a drain of a clog by taking off the pipes underneath the sink, I had never done it. Time for faith in action! I got out the tools, crawled under the sink, and looked upward at a smiling God. He knew all along what was best for me!

Faith powered works breed success! Continue to do good for others, but with your heart behind what you do. That is God's way.

How have you put faith in action?

Further study: Hebrews 6:10

Day 2

Let There Be Light!

Now faith is being sure of what we hope for and certain of what we do not see. This is what the ancients were commended for. Hebrews 11:1-2

Pastor Bob was negotiating with the bank for a loan to finish the new church building. Every night as he pulled up the covers and drifted off to sleep, visions of business plans, financial statements, assets, and liabilities danced in his head. Bob had been doing the breaststroke in paperwork to secure the building loan for the church as well as juggling his demanding job as a probation officer. He was meeting with the financial institution for the third time about a loan. Understanding church financing seemed to be out of their arena.

"We always get enough to pay the bills!" he told the banker.

"How?" The banker wanted to know as he gazed around at the shell of the unfinished building.

"Faith! God provides! We operate by faith!"

"That may be, Pastor Bob, but faith isn't good enough for the corporate office."

After a pause, the banker reconsidered, "Well, I guess we do. We loan money, and have faith people will repay it!" Within a few weeks, the bank issued the very first loan ever for a church. About the same time, the old chapel sold for cash. It had been on the market so long some began to lose hope, and money helped with the unfinished building.

Soon afterwards when funds purchased basic materials, Bob realized the church needed lights. He called the church treasurer to ask about money for the fixtures. "There's no money for that, Bob," Sandy told him.

Bob responded cheerfully, “God always provides. I’m asking him now for lights! Then I’m going to the post office to pick up the mail.”

A check tumbled out of one envelope. It was for $5000! The letter inside from a single mom explained all. During the raging forest fire when she was one of more than 26,000 evacuated from homes and jobs, she lost so much pay she couldn’t pay her mortgage one month and feed her family as well. Though she had been a stranger, our church paid her mortgage. She continued in her letter, “When my father died, we sold his house. I am sending you the tithe on my share from the sale.”

Bob called the treasurer that afternoon “God always provides, but we turn our back on him when we don’t ask!”

He headed to the home improvement store, the pastor looking forward to bringing *God’s light* as well as *God’s light fixtures* to the congregation the next Sunday!

What can you ask of God in faith today?

Further study: Hebrews 11:4-40

Day 3

Moving Mountains, One Recycled Can at a Time

"I tell you the truth, if you have the faith as small as a mustard seed, you can say to this mountain, 'Move from here to there' and it will move. Nothing will be impossible for you." Matthew 17:20-21

It was December 10, the year I had given notice I would be resigning from a tiny rural school staff in southern Arizona in May and moving. Little details were still open, like where we were moving and where I would teach the following year.

Lance and Travis had handed me illustrated letters to Santa. Each boy had drawn himself riding a new mountain bike, detailing the color and model wanted so there would be no mistake. Christmas was fifteen days away, and my sons wanted bikes that cost as much as groceries for our family of three for over two months! "Boys," I began, "I can tell you for sure that Santa is NOT going to bring you mountain bikes this Christmas." The protests started right away.

"But we need them!"

"Yes you do," I agreed, "and you can *earn them*."

"It will take too long! We'll be in high school by then!" one chimed.

"Yeah," the other wailed, "I'll be driving my own Toyota Four-Runner by the time we have the money for new bikes!"

In the midst of labeled boxes packed and stacked along the hall and in each closet, I thought about my big step of faith of moving into the unknown. It was time for the twins to also learn how to move mountains—or mountain bikes—with faith.

I offered a game plan. Aluminum cans. The two groaned. We never bought soda or anything in recyclable cans, but there were plenty of cans scattered around. Driving out on the desert with trash sacks, I remarked that the area would be greatly improved by can pick-up! The boys were not enthusiastic.

Soon, people in the community began to notice. One gave the boys a 55-gallon drum of cans, and another donated a refrigerator box of cans. On the first trip to town to cash them in, the boys were jammed together in the single passenger seat because of the size of our aluminum load, all smelling like Whiskey Row. When the crumpled bills hit Travis' and Lance's hands, they both began to hope and believe. The first load was a third of the price of one bicycle. "Wow!" exclaimed Travis. "We'll be able to get bikes after all." After that, we worked on making jewelry together to sell at a campground crafts show, and made money from a moving sale with their undersized bunk beds and small bicycles. Now they had all the money, and would buy the new bicycles when we got to our new destination.

Our mustard seeds of faith had grown to the size of watermelons as the boys and I made the trip to the large store to purchase their bicycles.

As the twins each carried a new helmet and rolled their new bikes up to the counter to pay for them, the cashier was as excited as they were to see them pay with their own money.

Seeds of faith can start very small and grow from there. Remember that all see you in steps of faith, and it can help someone believe!

How can you encourage another's faith?

Further study: Romans 4:16-21

Day 4
All This For Minor Surgery?

"Be still and know that I am God." Psalm 46:10

"Fixing the damage from childbirth is routine, simple, and easier than getting a haircut," the surgeon assured me. He explained that it is fairly common for women to be ripped like the veil in the Temple when giving birth, especially when nearly fifteen pounds of bouncing baby boys had been involved. Ordinary and common as it was, I was still nervous about the operation.

Preparing to leave on the 200 mile trip to the city just after sunup had me packing Mom's and my suitcases in the car and arranging for her to stay in a hotel for two nights so she could drive me home. Lastly, we arranged for friends to check on the twins to make sure they didn't run out of pizza or bandages.

All was ready the evening before when the phone rang. It was a cheerful voice from the hospital. "This is Candy from the Blah Blah Hospital. I see you have surgery scheduled tomorrow for ..." and she named off the technical description. She continued without emotion, moving right into preparation for death and dissection. "We have a copy of your will and the health care power of attorney, which is required. I also see on your records that you are an organ donor."

She paused, "Say, just what organs do you plan to donate?"

I felt the fear rise in the hair on my neck. Just how minor was this surgery? Then I remembered the Psalm shown above: "Be still and know I am God." And Psalm 46:11 that follows with the promise "The LORD Almighty is with us; the God of Jacob is our fortress."

As Mom and I traveled to the city for my surgery, I knew there were three of us in the car—one was God!

Recall a time of uncertainty. How did you realize God was with you?

Further study: Psalm 56:3-4

Day 5
The Bear Box

Some trust in chariots and some in horses, but we trust in the name of the Lord *our God.* Psalm 20:7

Excitement spread as the family headed to Yosemite, a long way from Bob and Glenda's desert home. Their sons, John, 5, and Jeff, 6, caught sight of the shady wooded campsite and cried together, "Wow! This is a '10'!"

Near the picnic table was something none but Bob had ever seen before: a heavy metal box with a hasp. "A bear box," Bob told Glenda. The boys were fascinated. While Bob was busy stringing tent poles together and Glenda made lunch, they hardly noticed when Jeff announced triumphantly, "John, you get in the bear box so the bears can't get you."

The campground strong box had been designed for food and other items with a strong smell that could attract bears, such as toothpaste and shampoo. To John and Jeff, the metal box captivated them as a new campsite amenity. From then until nightfall, the boys practiced for hours playing in the bear box. First one boy went inside, then the other. But neither closed the heavy door and twisted the hasp.

The next morning, Bob and Glenda were busy packing up the car before 7:00 and they didn't notice their boys practicing with the empty bear box for the last time. This time, though, Jeff crawled inside and his younger brother, John, closed the lid and twisted the hasp. Then John wondered aloud in a quiet voice, "Now how do I get this unlocked?"

Jeff, inside the metal compartment, panicked, "AAAH! AAAAH! Help!" His screaming rang through the forest and bounced off the trees. Though Glenda rushed over to turn the hasp and free Jeff so he could escape, the boy walked with shaky knees to the car.

After a quick conference with his dad, John yelled, "Hey, Jeff! I know how to use a bear box now!" But Jeff didn't move from the back seat.

God is with us, as he promises. No matter how fearful any circumstance is, whether physical, mental or emotional, or one involving someone we care about, we can trust that God is with us forever and always.

What frightening circumstance has worried you or someone you care about?

Will you give it to God today?

Further study: 1 Samuel 20:1-42

Day 6

Just How Deep is the Water?

Save me, O God, for the waters have come up to my neck. Psalm 69:1

Teenager Chris, the twins and I, boarded the ferry boat to travel over to Vancouver Island in British Columbia, Canada. It was a new experience for the three of them. For Chris, it was yet another adventure forging through the unknown with crazy Aunt Jo. I'm sure Chris thought of me as Sacagawea, guiding him and the twins through the Pacific Northwest just as Lewis and Clark had done a century before.

"After three weeks of traveling and camping together, isn't this great, having hot food we don't have to cook and dishes we don't have to wash?" I looked around to see who agreed. The twins, their mouths surrounded by crumbs, nodded. Chris gripped the edge of his padded seat with white knuckles. He wasn't appreciating the pincushion wooded islands on the blue water that were a stunning change from his desert home, where he had lived since birth.

"What can he be so afraid of?" I wondered. Perhaps Chris, being raised in a land-locked area, had never seen so much water. As the ferry's motors rumbled and tickled his feet with the vibration on the steel deck, Chris let go of the seat and began to pace. Then he announced, "I'm going to take a walk around the outside." The twins and I watched him and noticed Chris stopped at each group of lifeboats.

When he returned, Chris asked me, "How deep is the water here anyway?" Chris peered at the water. "I've counted them. They don't have enough lifeboats for all of us!" A half-hour later when we landed at the island, I wondered if Chris stumbled when we got off the ferry, or had he stopped to kiss the solid ground?

Some people have so much anxiety that it affects their walk with the Lord.

Do you feel that the waters around you are too deep? I do at times. A good strategy is to pray through worry. What if, during prayer, you breathe in Jesus and breathe out your fears?

Further study: 2 Samuel 22:31-37; Psalm 70:1-4

Day 7

Let's Hear It for Bionic Women!

Stand firm, then, with the belt of truth buckled around your waist, with the breastplate of righteousness in place, and with your feet fitting with the readiness that comes from the gospel of peace.

Ephesians 6:14-15

To say that it had been a bad week at work for me was like saying that the Titanic had only weighed as much as a steam iron. I thought about changing my weekend plans. My life had dropped into an abyss, and no exotic recipe using chocolate could get me to climb out of my personal black hole.

Still, Imogene and I had planned to travel to a nearby community for its annual family footrace or race walk competition. For us, it was not to win, but as a statement of renewed health! Just five months before at a much earlier age than most, I had had a total knee replacement.

Before my bionic knee, I had race walked the course several times with runners of all ages from up to 200 miles away. I had always admired the grandparents running with their grandchildren in the shorter race, and older adults trotting along effortlessly behind the lead truck in a 10 K over the wide plains dotted with stunted desert green foliage.

If I had been looking for an excuse to skip the race, I could find it in the late November weather, which was feisty and cold with snow predicted.

"Let's do it anyway!"

Imogene almost sang the words. Sometimes her knees hurt, too. "Nevah give in!" Winston Churchill had commanded in a famous 1941 speech. After all, if we gave up because of little things like stress and wind, we would be conceding we had an overdose of age and "rheumatiz." Nope. Couldn't do that.

We rose at a windy sunrise with the cold slicing at us like knives. As Imogene and I traveled to get there, we saw skies dark with a storm penciling in streaks on the red mesas in the distance.

The pistol fired, signaling the start! Imogene and I walked along briskly, talking and laughing with many passing us. At the finish line, Imogene rushed ahead with a camera to capture me crossing the line, my arms raised in victory. First in the knee replacement class! All other awards were minor.

Over the hill group? Never! Just faith-filled women!

Our faith is built in small blocks with memories and experiences cementing it together. Is your faith where you want or need it today? If not, have patience with yourself as God has with you.

Further study: Romans 1:17; Proverbs 3:5-6

Questions

Put Your Money Where Your Mouth Is

Except for the thin air, I would prefer that all of my life was made up of mountaintop experiences. But it isn't. A suggestion from a clergyman to a family man out of work and in extreme financial circumstances was to begin a "What I love about my life" journal.

He suggested these categories to consider:

What I love

- about my life today about being (married, single, widowed)
- about my family and children
- about my job (retirement or other circumstances)
- about my God

It is another way of counting your blessings! What evidence of stepping out in faith can you see in your life?

How has your faith or outlook affected others?

Reflections:

A Bible in the hand is worth
two on the shelf.

Week 12

Is Our God Big Enough to Trust for an Epidemic Flu and an Empty Bank Account?

Day 1

Any Doctors Give a Group Discount?

Ask and it will be given to you, seek and you will find, knock and the door will be opened to you. For everyone who asks, receives; he who seeks, finds, and to him who knocks, the door will be opened.

Matthew 7:7

"How are the kids today?" Sam asked when he called his wife, Angie.

"Cheryl is sick and Marie has the sniffles. I'll take them to the doctor today after work," Angie said.

"Another doctor visit, another bill," Sam thought. The couple had had a tight budget when they married, but after the children came—three in close succession—the last thing either wanted to hear was that one of their children had to go to the doctor.

The next day, young Randy had a high fever. The boy couldn't go to school that day. Sam took their son to the doctor before he reported for work. "Another doctor visit, another bill equal to groceries for two days," Sam thought in exasperation.

Payday to payday seemed to make no difference. There was nothing left after doctor bills but crumbs and dirty laundry. Had God picked out their household for one of the plagues of Egypt?

Angie sponged their son's forehead and spooned down medicine. Later, as they settled into bed, Angie suggested, "Sam, I think it would be cheaper if we paid our tithe!" So they pledged that God would get the first offering, and everything else would be paid after that. Soon after, Sam and Angie noticed that surprise checks began arriving in their mailbox just when their family needed them.

What is the idea behind tithing?

Further study: Luke 21:1-4

Day 2

Hair-Raising Compliments

"Be careful not to do your 'acts of righteousness' before men, to be seen by them. If you do, you will have no reward from your Father in heaven."

Matthew 6:1

I had talked my beautician into perming my hair for the latest and easiest style. Though it might have seemed like overkill because my hair is scrub-pad curly in damp weather, I had longed for a style that would be in perfect order for work with just seconds of care. No more would I have tangled locks to cut free from a brush nor have to tie it into a pony tail to tame the tendrils! The treatment had been expensive, and it had been totally different from anything I had ever tried. I could hardly wait to hear what my teen sons thought.

As I put dinner on the table, I patted my puffy curly locks, still smelling of perm. Each glanced up, but only to ask, "Any seconds?" and "Is there any dessert?" At the end of the meal when my young men's plates were clean, I had to ask, "Well, what do you think of the hair? You haven't said anything about it."

Lance put both hands in the air and reported, "God says, 'This is my daughter, in whom I am well pleased. But the FRO has got to GO!'"

Years later, when I went blonde and flew up to see my sons for a week, I was not surprised that neither twin said anything about the change. However, I knew I changed the hair for myself, not for compliments.

Similarly, when we honor God with our offerings, our talents, gifts, and time, it is between God and us. We are not doing it for public applause. So, if I am disturbed by recipients of my gifts who neither acknowledged nor thanked me in any way, I had to ask myself why I gave a gift. Was it for a pat on the back or for them? When I give to God, is it to be rewarded or because I love him?

What is your reason for giving?

Further study: John 3:21

Day 3
Stop! Thief!

> *Give generously to him and do so without a grudging heart, then because of this, the* L*ORD your God will bless you in all your work and in everything you put your hand to.* Deuteronomy 15:10

Charley was thrilled to share his life with Liz, a kind Christian woman who brought light and beauty into his life. His heart sang to be with her, and Charley would follow her anywhere, even to her Christian church. Liz was eager to teach him.

"Let's go to church together Sunday," Liz suggested. Charley figured this would give him points with her and her family.

"Sure," he responded, "then I'll take you out to lunch! I have a special place in mind." Attending church while they were dating became part of their lives, and it continued when they married.

Liz told her new husband, "We need to set aside our tithe." That was something new.

After she explained what a tithe was, Charley wondered why anyone in their right mind would give so much of their earnings. "This has to be like throwing it in the Black Hole." Still, he got out an envelope and grudgingly put the cash in, grumbling to himself, "That sure seems like a lot of money we could use for other things."

Going out for an afternoon drive one day, he and Liz returned home to see disruption and disorder in their tidy house! Someone had broken in and gone through drawers, closets, cupboards, and dumped everything on the floor!

As the newlyweds put things back in order together and determined what was missing, Charley cried in surprise, "Whadda ya know? Nothing is missing except the envelope with the cash tithe in it!" Charley continued, "I guess God thought the burglar needed the money more than he or we did! That means we're off the hook!"

"That's not the way it works, Sweetheart." With patience, Liz taught her new husband that the tithe wasn't paid until it reached its intended location. They both made up the missing cash and took it to church the next week.

God loves generous and cheerful givers. How have you been blessed with a tithe offering?

Further study: Psalm 20:3-4

Day 4

Who Gets the First Cookie?

Be sure to give a tenth of all that your fields produce each year. Eat the tithe of your grain, new wine and oil, and the firstborn of your herds and flocks in the presence of the Lord your God at the place he will choose as a dwelling for his Name, so that you may learn to revere the Lord your God always.

Deuteronomy 14:22-23

"Eric, take these cookies to your brother Jim. Tell him I love him and will see him soon." During this busy summer, Jim and Janet's work schedules, time and distance made face-to-face meetings difficult. The box of her best cookies was a love offering until they could meet again. They had set their wedding date for the next summer.

Janet dropped a card in the top of the box. Eric noticed her lipstick kiss on the back of the envelope.

"How corny!" he thought, rolling his eyes. "I'll never be that way when I fall in love."

Eric thought about the box next to him as he drove over a hundred miles to his job and to Jim. The box was the size of four gallons of milk. Inside were dozens of cookies carefully packed in layers with paper in between. Everyone agreed: Jim's fiancée, Janet, was the best cook in the county. This batch of "everything cookies" were full of chocolate, M and M's, several kinds of nuts, and fresh vanilla.

Sending Eric with the cookies was like sending an alcoholic on a cross country trip with a case of liquor beside him. The unmarried man hardly cooked and never baked.

Eric could smell the fresh-baked sweetness. He wondered, "I just bet they're soft and chewy." The chocolate was calling to him. Who would notice if he ate a few cookies off the top layer? He tried one. Then he took another. Soon the top later was empty down to the paper, so he took that evidence off, crumpled it and hid the paper in his trash bag.

Two weeks later, Jim and Janet were able to meet again. "How did you like the cookies?" Janet asked, her eyes twinkling.

Jim was truly puzzled. "What cookies?" Janet told him about the box she sent with his brother.

Then Jim remembered that his brother came up with two fabulous cookies he shared from a box of crumbs. Eric said he got the treats "from somewhere."

Eric had been expected to give the cookie love offering to his brother first, just as we honor God by giving to him first. Do we give God the first or the last cookie?

Give a portion to God first and everything else will fall into place. It may seem that with challenges and bills, we have to hold back, but as we trust God with our needs and bills by giving to him first, we learn how well He takes care of us.

It doesn't make sense in our world to give without knowing how to meet the daily challenges, but in God's world, it does make sense.

We can never know just how many surprises come our way until we try putting God first.

How has God astonished you with windfalls?

Further study: 1 Samuel 2 and 3

Day 5
A Gift Given

You are to give them the firstfruits of your grain, new wine and oil, and the first wool from the shearing of your sheep. Deuteronomy 18:4

The empty classroom still held the magic of Christmas, and I had left the tree lights twinkling. The children had left for Christmas break. I was touched by so many presents adding color and a festive look to my desk. I opened each one, thinking of how special each child was to me and how thoughtful they had chosen a gift to share. I was touched by the mom and daughter who gave me a three-foot teddy holding ice skates. Not only was the grocery store the only place to shop for thirty-five miles, but the girl's father had just left her mom and her to be on their own. Now all but two students were being raised in single parent families.

As I wrote thank you notes, modeling letter writing I taught them, I turned over one gift—a china headed doll. I remembered the child handing me the package and saying, "This is for you!" On the tag, it read, "To Clare from Grandma." In her home, because of poverty, I knew this gift was one she picked out from her own and she wanted to share it with me. The gift was like the widow who gave all she had—three mites—as an offering.

But what if we opened a gift from an adult who had money enough to buy gifts and we found it addressed, "To Sylvia, Love, Tom," and we aren't Sylvia? When you give God your first gift by writing the first check as your tithe, you are honoring your creator. If you know how you feel being given a gift that had been given to someone else, how does God rate your gift if you do the same thing?

How have you trusted him with what you have? How has he given back to you?

Further study: Philippians 4:19

Day 6

Whistle While You Work!

> *Remember this: Whoever sows sparingly will also reap sparingly, and whoever sows generously will also reap generously. Each man should give what he has decided in his heart to give, not reluctantly or under compulsion, for God loves a cheerful giver.*
>
> 2 Corinthians 9:6-7

"I can't believe you're painting this house for free!" Nick commented high on a ladder above me. Normally, this job and the preparation would pay in the four-figure range. As we painted, the owner of the house, Denise, was at Mayo Clinic fighting for her life.

Nick's wife, Ruth, on a second ladder, turned to see what I would say. The three of us were finishing the paint on the two-story log house in a wooded neighborhood.

The paint could not be rolled on or sprayed because of the condition of the house and the curves of the logs. It had to be hand painted with brushes as wide as telephone books.

"I'm not doing it for free. I'm doing it for God!"

Nick laughed out loud. He and Ruth earned their living painting and roofing houses. When their chuckles stopped rocking the two ladders, he said, "Well, I sure hope God is paying you for this!"

"Yep!" I told him, "he already did."

I told him how a mistake from my mortgage company yielded a large windfall check the week before.

Would Denise survive the cancer? Only God knew. I did know that she needed the paint job to preserve the house, whether she won this battle or not. If she didn't make it, her daughter, Erica, would have less work to get the house ready to sell.

I'd handled two family members' deaths and estates in a year, and then lost the rest of the generation within six months. I know handling estates is complicated and time-consuming. Long distance makes it harder, and Erica lives far away. Her mother is her only parent.

Was I a cheerful giver? Sure! The three of us enjoyed this mild summer day in the shade of evergreen trees all afternoon and finished the painting job. Denise came back to a home makeover, and she recovered to attend her daughter's wedding.

Whatever your talents, God will nudge you to use them. See what surprises come from following his way!

What of your talents can God use?

Further study: 2 Corinthians 9:10-12

Day 7

Where is Jesus When You Expect Him?

> *Honor the* L*ORD* *with your wealth, with the firstfruits of all your crops; then all your barns will be filled to overflowing, and your vats will brim over with new wine.* Proverbs 3:9-10

Five-year-old Maria was just learning how to give. Her mother, Sharon, helped Maria count and divide her allowance from doing chores at home. The new coins from the bank sparkled like toys.

"See, Maria. We're going to give Jesus ten percent. This is how we do it. For each dollar, we give Jesus a dime. That's this little silver coin."

Maria helped with the next two dollars, finding two dimes for Jesus.

"We'll wrap it up in this little bag and have it ready for Sunday," Sharon said. "Then you can give it to Jesus on Sunday."

Maria was thrilled! Just imagine meeting Jesus, who would love these sparkly coins!

Sunday came, and Maria clutched her little bag for Jesus money tightly.

The grown-ups talked and talked. Then Maria went to the children's class.

Some guys showed up with a popcorn bowl. None had a beard like Jesus. The teacher put a piece of paper in the bowl.

Maria still clutched her bag, and wondered, "When will Jesus show up?"

After the service, Sharon noticed Maria was still holding tight to her bag of coins.

"What happened, Sweetie? You didn't give your money to Jesus!"

"I was going to, Mom, but he didn't show up!"

Teaching your children to tithe and doing so yourself completes a cycle of love.

God doesn't need our money. He owns all creation.

Instead, to me, tithing is a payback for all the years of uncertainty when God gave my little family all that we needed. I had a job when my employer was downsizing, manageable repairs on the house and car while raising my sons, and gas for small adventure trips.

God's bounty really kicked in one time when a stranger donated half a beef to our family when the freezer hosted only a fresh-wrapped catch of ice cubes.

Though the stranger who gave us half a beef never went to any church, he was God's messenger in showing love for us. He gave from what he had: his herd.

How can we not return God's caring favor?

Further study: Luke 10:30-37; The Good Samaritan

Questions

Is Our God Big Enough to Trust for an Epidemic Flu and an Empty Bank Account?

Tithe Blessing Cards can start with a pack of index cards that cost less than a buck. They tally a list which reflects how and when God has blessed you. When I took a fifty percent pay cut moving out of an isolated teaching post with free housing, utilities, and a generous bonus for "hardship pay," I began writing down dates and blessings that God brought to us. When our family's needs were greater, the blessings came more frequently—sometimes every day. When the needs were less, the surprises were less frequent. In the child-rearing days, the gifts had included surprise checks in the mail, sixty pounds of venison, cases of food, free trees to plant, three service trips to the tire/brake shop with the owner waiving the charge, and tax refunds. In later times, the blessings had looked like a free service call on the temperamental gas heater that could not seem to make it through winter, medical care with the co-pay waived, gift cards, and sales bonuses. Want to know who is the best philanthropist? God.

Describe your attitude about tithing and its benefits.

____

____

____

____

____

____

____

How can you honor God and help others with a gift of your time?

____

____

____

____

Reflections:

____

____

____

____

____

____

____

From what we get, we can make a living;
What we give, however, makes a life.

Arthur Ashe

Week 13

Trust in God, Goals and Your Dishrag

Day 1

Trust in God and Your Dishrag

My son, if you accept my words and store up my commands within you, turning your ear to wisdom and applying your heart to understanding, and if you call out for insight and cry aloud for understanding and if you look for it as for silver and search for it as for hidden treasure, then you will understand the fear of the Lord and find the knowledge of God.

Proverbs 2:1-5

Do you ever long for something that was and is no more? A lost love? A favorite pet? I long for my old dishwasher that rumbled like a tank idling in the kitchen.

For nearly a decade, the dishwasher sterilized mountains of dirty dishes, soiled garden trowels, oily tools, and rubber garden sandals. It seemed divinely blessed, like the Israelites' relationship to God in the times of Prophet Samuel.

I nearly wiped a tear remembering the "tank" never needed service.

Just as God's people traded their creator for a tall, handsome, rich king, I was so carried away with all the new dishwasher features, I forgot the "tank." Stainless steel interior? Great idea. Delayed start? Half load option. Oh, Wow! Quieter? Absolutely!

Once the new dishwasher with dials, features, and a 100-page instruction book was installed by a professional, I put it to work right away. The machine sloshed almost silently all over the dishes. It cost three times as much as the tank.

Did it work three times as well as the old one? The glasses were smudgy with milk film and fingerprints. I ran the dishwasher again. Not much improvement. Some loads were better than others.

After black flecks decorated everything in the dishwasher, I looked way down in with the silverware, and wondered "How did that teabag get in there?" I was careful about tea after that. Then there was the white powdery something inside the dark cups.

The young repairman bent over the filter drain and emptied it. "You know you have to wash the dishes first right?"

"Well, rinse them off. I did that." He explained that his mother taught him that the dishwasher is for *sanitizing* the dishes. To wash them first was next to Godliness. "It makes the dishwasher last longer."

"You're not washing the dishes well enough before you put them in," the repairman advised me. I felt like this young judge had just sentenced me to a decade of washing dishes.

So my new prima dona dishwasher has forced me to wash dishes by hand to perfection so that it can sanitize them.

Just as the Israelites did after Saul was king, I long for the old relationship. I'm learning patience, appreciation, and thankfulness, I guess. I don't let the dishes pile up on the counter.

I'd taken "the tank" for granted like when we forget the wonderful gifts that God gives us every day. In the meantime, I dream of the day the prima donna wears out.

Have you thanked God for life's blessings today?

Further study: 1 Samuel 10-1 Samuel 16

Day 2

When You Boys are Grown and Gone!

"For this reason, a man will leave his father and mother and be united to his wife, and the two will become one flesh." Ephesians 5:31

God gives us teenagers so we have the courage to cut the umbilical cord.

In fact, after a few years in the double digits, we don't have a scalpel, but a bayonet ready and a calendar with big X's. We're trying to survive with a non-additive pacifier (like chocolate). A slogan helps. For many mothers, it might be, "This, too, shall pass."

For me, it was, "When you boys are grown and gone!"

As a new mother, I was charmed with my twins, remembering all the sweet experiences of those little feet. Christmas was special. So were lost teeth, homemade Mother's Day gifts, their hope, and happiness. I glowed when they said, "Mom, I love you berry mucsh!" I still do.

Then my offspring turned thirteen. Love was reserved for girls and French fries, not moms. Moms *never* bought them the things they wanted. It was embarrassing to be in the company of a senior citizen like you. You were interfering. They rolled their eyes often. It wasn't because the eye doctor prescribed the exercise.

When I came home from work for lunch to find one sweaty son pedaling on a bike stand in the living room, I asked,

"What are you doing home?"

"I thought you knew I got suspended for a few days."

Of course I didn't. He took the notice out of the mail box.

"When you boys are grown and gone, I will...."

When I paid their woodshop class bill and asked them to make a mudroom bench, the two came home with three dogsleds. The third sled was a masterpiece in oak. You couldn't sit on it while taking off muddy shoes or park it in the hallway. Oh, well.

Later, after a heated argument about slavery and oppression, one said, "I just bet you can hardly wait for us to move out!"

"You're right. When you boys are grown and gone, I will have a great time throwing parties and the yard will look like *Sunset Magazine*!"

God does this on purpose because letting go also means that the rules change. The kids do leave home, and then the mom rules change.

My sons got married. I figured the family just got bigger. I was wrong.

I'm not the head of the family any more. I had to step back with respect to their new bonded relationship with their wives.

God had made two into one. That means Moms now have to take a different role. They need to be less demanding.

They must:

- hold back on tips and advice unless asked.
- respect the couple their children have become.
- ask permission instead of taking over.
- give the new family space.
- let them create their own traditions.

It's God's way, and the right way.

"When you boys are grown and gone…" I remembered. They remembered, too, and we laugh. I do have parties and a yard that looks like *Sunset Magazine,* but my new role of mom is letting go to let their love grow.

How have you given your children boundaries and wings?

Further study: Proverbs 3:13-18

Day 3

Where Everything Says Welcome

In my Father's house are many rooms; if it were not so, I would have told you. I am going there to prepare a place for you. And if I go and prepare a place for you, I will come back and take you to be with me that you also may be where I am. John 14:2-4

"Is this punishment? Why are you giving me this listing? In that neighborhood, the residents shoot first and ask questions later! The house hasn't been painted since Eisenhower was president. It looks like it was built by school kids!"

"Look for the good in it! This will be a good experience for you! You can really prove yourself as a sales professional," replied the broker.

So Adelle punched down the "lock" button for all her doors and angrily drove to the house that morning, her knuckles white on the steering wheel. "This is a realtor's nightmare!" she thought as she passed by familiar buildings on the way. The years and suburbs had taken a toll on the neighborhood. In fact, it wasn't far from where she herself had been raised. She could recall how it had looked. Now it was the slums.

Then Adelle noticed that though the stucco had fallen in patches from the peeling blue house, it looked over the creek with a dirt bike path along the bank, giving the residents a more spacious yard and view.

The homeowners had noticed, too. They had arranged lawn chairs on the porch to face the creek. Under the shade of generous trees was a freshly painted miniature chair, just the right size for a grandchild. The lawn was green and thick, freshly cut, and the crooked wire gate was wide open for all to enter.

Adelle's nose caught the wonderful aroma of a familiar dish simmering on the stove. Someone had started cooking very early. She closed her eyes, remembering the taste, and how it often meant that the family had gathered around the table together to eat.

"Why, everything about this place says 'Welcome'!" she realized.

The welcoming feel to a home may not come in a theatre room or a kitchen built especially for entertaining. Instead, a home's setting may be full of surprises, just like God.

Jesus surprised the Israelites showing up as a carpenter. They were expecting an imposing and powerful military commander, possibly entering the scene in a chariot pulled by a pair of matched horses, and with an archer along. Instead, Jesus gathered attention over thousands with his love, words, and glance. His hands healed physical and mental illnesses, and well as broken people.

Though the shabby house is not what the world considers worthwhile, it offers genuine love and welcome. Jesus always offers us love and a welcome home.

How do you make others feel welcome?

Further study: John 13:1-15

Day 4
Got Water?

Let your ear be attentive and your eyes open to hear the prayer your servant is praying before you day and night for your servants, the people of Israel.
Nehemiah 1:6

Who would have thought that taking a shower would be such a luxury and a challenge? Although I had determined ahead of time my summer in Alaska would be the adventure of my life, I did not realize that taking a sponge bath in a soup bowl of water warmed on the stove would be the norm. Most cabins where I lived or house-sat were without running water. The summer I retired from teaching, I flew to Alaska to work for a resort hotel during the tourist season to be near my sons for a time.

One late summer scorcher, a coworker complained in the employee lounge, "I'll be glad when winter gets here. I just can't stand the heat!"

"But Carol," I remarked from an Arizonan's view, "It is only 53 degrees!"

"That's what I mean! It's just too stinking hot!"

So it was when I stayed in one house with running water, I tried running the tap to heat it up, but couldn't get it above iceberg temperature in five minutes. It could drain the water holding tank before warming. So I just soaped up, jumped in with a gasp, turned around and jumped out.

My Alaska shower can compared to my prayer life. Do we just jump in, turn around and jump out? Or, is our prayer time deliberate like Nehemiah's described above?

Nehemiah did not stop praying for several days. He also mourned for his people and did not eat. He apologized for their sins and his own. All his focus was on praying and reconnecting with God.

What difference would doubling our prayer time make in our spiritual life?

Further study: Luke 18:1-8

Day 5

The Best Birthday

I have set the L*ORD* *always before me. Because he is at my right hand, I will not be shaken.* Psalm 16:8

At the family college dorm where the boys and I lived during the summers while I went to school, forty or so children crowded into the roomy clubhouse to celebrate yet another birthday. It was the third one that week. The decorations were different, the parents, and the gifts, but the small guests were the same. "Whose birthday is it today?" one boy had asked another. "I dunno, but the cake is good!" "Yeah, and look at the cool toys he got." They had been rolling trucks around that belonged to the birthday boy—whoever he was.

Lance and Travis would soon turn eight, and I did not want another cookie-cutter birthday at the clubhouse. I reasoned out the time for an outdoor party based on the monsoon summer rain schedule. I picked our favorite city park with covered cabanas for shelter in case of rain. All that week, you could have set your watch by the drenching monsoon rains that poured at 2:00 p.m., and then shut off like a faucet after an hour. By 3:30, there would be no signs it had ever rained. I set the party time for 4:00 p.m.

Birthday day came. It was a heart-warming sight to see clear skies at noon, then 1:00 p.m. more entirely blue skies, and at 2:00 p.m., more sunshine. At three o-clock, the clouds began to form. By three-thirty, they looked pretty heavy and black. Mom showed up to help drive kids to the park, "Not to be making noises like a mother, but why don't we have the party at the dorm? All the kids will be meeting here and it will be dry indoors."

"Too impersonal!" I told her. "We are going to the park."

The eight guests and rain arrived together, precisely at 3:45. I had some of the guests in my car and my mom had the rest in her small sedan. As she followed me, the rain turned to hail, banging on the hood and bouncing like popcorn. My guests were delighted, deciding this was better than the movies. In my rear-view mirror, I could see Mom's grim face. With her mouth cheerlessly drawn like a line across her face, she looked like a fair weather outdoor enthusiast.

As we turned off to the park, the rain slowed to a sprinkle. As I parked, the last drip of rain squeezed out of the sky, and all the boys shouted with glee and amazement as they rushed out of the car, "Wow! We're the only ones here!" It was as if the popular park had been reserved just for our party. Tall pines dripped with rain, freshly bathed. Puddles on the basketball court mirrored puffy, light clouds and a blue sky.

We enjoyed the birthday feast under a dry cabana. Later, all the boys tried out the new T-ball set. Joyful voices bounced off the trees as the guests and birthday boys slid on the slippery pine needles. There was no doubt whose birthday it was after all. It was the very best ever.

Part of motherhood is not being shaken no matter what happens.

Perhaps inside, we do not feel as confident and steady as we look on the outside, but God is with us. Practicing being calm inside and continuing to trust in the Lord is a worthy goal.

When you feel shaken, what works for you?

Further study: Job 2:10; Psalm 15:1-2

Day 6

What Exercise Do You Do?

All Scripture is God-breathed and is useful for teaching, rebuking, correcting and training in righteousness. 2 Timothy 3:16

Caroline had not seen Jeane for some years as she stopped by to see her one sunny spring day when the palm trees waved in the warm air. "Oh, Jeane! Getting older isn't for sissies. Now I have to pick pants and skirts with elastic waists. Whatever happened to us? But you have stayed so slender!"

Jeane did not have much of a battle because of fruits and veggies in the refrigerator. Also, she had been ill. However, she skirted exercise completely.

"Jeane, how do you stay so slim? What exercises do you do?" When Caroline drove up, she had noticed that Jeane lived across the street from the condo clubhouse and swimming pool. She guessed that with Jeane's short sporty haircut, she swam often.

Wrong. She had never been in the pool.

"Well," Jeane shared pointing to a stack of books on the table next to her, "I like to read. Turning the pages is all the exercise I get!"

Spiritual exercise is like Jeane's love of reading. We get stronger as we practice praying, studying the Bible, trusting God with all the impossible issues, serving others' needs and giving of ourselves. These strategies equip us for all of life as well as God's work.

How much spiritual growth have you experienced through a daily walk with God?

Further study: Psalm 115:12-13

Day 7
The Godfather

Let us not give up meeting together, as some are in the habit of doing, but let us encourage one another.
Hebrews 10:25

Sheriff's Deputy Ron surprised guests at a wedding showing up at the house of worship for the ceremony, a place he usually considered as savory as a brawl at a bar. Ron knew the groom well and had made promises to the young man's parents, so he conceded to darken the door of a church.

One law enforcement colleague was taken aback at Ron's presence. "What are you doing here?"

Ron cleared his throat. He opened his coat, revealing a .357 magnum pistol in a shoulder holster. "I'm the Godfather!" Ron proclaimed.

"We are gathered here together…." The minister began.

The key is "we." Ron and others may say that they can meet God in a sunset, while boating, riding horses, playing golf, or during any other activity. Church is not in a building, but in meeting with others to worship. Being together helps to keep us on the path as God's children. As travelers on this earth, we are subject to all kinds of challenges.

Think of a slender wood barbeque skewer. By itself, how easy it is to break? What about with six sticks, ten, or a bundle? A group of worshipers can encourage, lift, and pray together, experiencing God's presence and love through any challenge. They are like an entire bundle of sticks, and strong in numbers. Though Ron felt uncomfortable inside a church, he could worship anywhere. When I lived one hundred miles from town, I had remembered the many places a group of us met to worship—in rickety folding chairs around the sparse shade of a desert tree, inside a hot bus converted to a chapel, under a picnic cabana, and inside of friends' homes. My family had attended Easter services on top of a rocky hill a long drive from home. Another Easter, all of us gathered in the shell of the new church. Its metal beams were exposed and both ends open on a freezing April morning for the first sunrise service in the unfinished building.

How do you worship today?

Further study: Psalm 86:8-10

Questions

Trust in God, Goals, and Your Dishrag.

The basics of spiritual growth are outlined in these simple steps:

1. Read your Bible daily
2. Attend church regularly
3. Get involved in a ministry group (Use your gifts to help others.)
4. Pray daily

These come from http://christianity.about.com.

Evaluate where you are in your spiritual life.

____

____

____

____

Where would you like to be with your spiritual life? Set specific action steps and a time line.

____

____

____

____

____

Reflections:

Footprints on the sands of time
are not made by sitting down.

Week 14

The Wow Factor of You—Before and After!

Day 1

A Wise Answer is Best

> *She is clothed with strength and dignity; she can laugh at the days to come. She speaks with wisdom and faithful instruction is on her tongue.*
>
> Proverbs 31:25-26

Mom knew just the right thing to do. For Mother's Day, she gave me three sheets of exterior siding. Other mothers might be thrilled with flowers and a dinner. This unusual gift made my heart jump for joy. With these four by eight sheets, the power saw, and some sheetrock, my teen sons and I could finish the sunroom we'd been building for weeks. It would mean the room would be weatherproof at last.

My tall twins were stapling up insulation inside and screwing sheetrock onto the ceiling. Working steadily, they could finish their part in less time than it took to cook a batch of pancakes. They invited their friends over, three teen brothers thirteen to seventeen years-old. As their macho and rusty pickup rolled into the driveway, I was thrilled to see that Nick, Trent, and Daniel brought a stereo as well as two cordless drills. They all braced and muscled up the heavy sheets. Their deep laughter rocked the unfinished room.

Then came the impasse. Drills stopped. The stereo blasted with the irreverent lyrics of a rock bank I hated. The five teens discussed ideas for a more exciting afternoon, and finishing the drywall wasn't even on the list.

Travis and Lance announced they were through working, PERIOD.

The two decided that child labor is illegal, and it could be fatal. I was starving them: they hadn't eaten in fifteen minutes. All felt faint.

To my request for anything, the answer was, "So?" Nothing worked to move through this: promises, threats, love, deals, and consequences. The question was, "Who cares?" The answer: Grandma. She had a summer home two miles away.

From birth to the present, she'd been a second parent to the twins. In a whole different way, whatever she said usually made a difference.

When Grandma called, I was up to my eyeballs in frustration. "I could just wring their necks," I told Mom through clenched teeth.

"I'll be right over," she quipped cheerfully.

Mom's handling of the teen revolt was wise and appropriate. She didn't look like a construction supervisor, but a grandma, with soft white hair and just the right tools tucked under her arm: a large package of cream-filled praline cookies!

"Oh, hi, Grandma!" Travis smiled with a bit of joy showing through.

"Are those for us?" Lance wanted to know. All ten eyes turned to see the luscious treats. The volume on the music quieted. This was the turning point.

Like God's just-right answers, hers also had an element of surprise. Soon, all four teens were whistling and working together. They finished the ceiling faster than the time it took to boil an egg. When the cookie package was empty and the work done, the five of them went off to enjoy a more adventurous afternoon.

I certainly had much to learn about forcing an issue. My mom used much wiser tactics right in line with the spiritual woman God wants us to be.

How often do we get so set on our own solution we don't consider any other? God has ways of gently moving us through challenges with solutions that we never considered. It's hands-on training! The key is to trust Him with the answer.

How has God helped you to be a better and wiser person?

Further study: John 13:34

Day 2

Help Wanted: One Personal White Knight

He defends the cause of the fatherless and the widow, and loves the alien, giving him food and clothing.
Deuteronomy 10:18

Margot screeched to a halt in front of a "nostalgia" shop, nearly bouncing her passenger, Jeane, off the dash. . Outside the bargain shop stood a full suit of armor on guard at the front door. Although the knight may have fit perfectly in a home with faux Spanish décor, the decoration now attracted attention to the shop.

"Now that's what every home needs," eighty-nine-year-old Margot announced.

"What's that?" Jeane wanted to know.

"See," Margot pointed to the metal guardian, "a knight in shining armor! That's the only way I'm going to get one!"

God cares for widows and fatherless children. Thanks to many who came forward to help at the time Margot and Jeane lost their lifelong partners, the widows adjusted to new responsibilities. The ladies grew with the changes and new roles in their lives.

We are the hands and feet of God. What responsibility can we take for those who need extra help?

Further study: James 1:27; Jeremiah 22:3

Day 3

God by Any Other Name is Good

O, Lord, you are my God; I will exalt you and praise your name, for in perfect faithfulness you have done marvelous things, things planned long ago.

Isaiah 25:1

The waiter brought a large steaming plate of onion rings and set them in the middle of the table where eight of us were enjoying a special dinner out. Remembering I had banned the delicious taste of onion rings at home along with most other fried food, I helped myself to the treat and was crunching away when the plate came by again. I picked up a fried and breaded piece that looked like a claw—certainly I had never seen an onion that shape!

"What is this?" I wanted to know.

"Why it's calamari!"

"What is calamari?"

"It's squid."

I then realized I had been eating tentacles, not onion rings!

I thought of other things which due to a bad reputation have been renamed for the purpose of marketing. For example, escargot disguises snails, pâté is made from ground up chicken livers, and "dried plums" gloss over the geriatric reputation of prunes.

While we have renamed things to gloss over ugly reputations, God's many names in the Old Testament continue to point out his power, love, leadership, and righteousness.

They are not names to hide God, but to describe him. *El Shaddai* means "God Almighty, the All Sufficient One," *Immanuel* means "God With Us," *Jehovah-Rohi* is "The Lord is My Shepherd,"

YHWH, "I AM. The one who is." *Jehovah-Rapha* translates to "The Lord who heals."

As you study the Bible and God's works and reflect on his presence, analyze where God is in your life now? Who is God to you?

Further study: Exodus 3:15

Day 4

Is God at Your Breakfast Table?

She watches over the affairs of her household and does not eat the bread of idleness. Her children arise and call her blessed; her husband also, and he praises her: "Many women do noble things, but you surpass them all." Proverbs 31:27-29

Prayer before meals, regular church attendance and training, and the boys writing "thank you" letters for gifts and requests to Santa—it was all part of the early years with my twins.

When the teen years came, ATTITUDE stepped up to home plate. I had enlisted the help of many stable couples at church to continue my sons' ongoing moral and spiritual growth. It had been a team effort. While I saw other parents let their growing children decide if they wanted to go to church, pray, or study the Bible, I didn't. Giving them a choice seemed to be something like the mom whose daughter flunked first grade reading and stood at the summer reading class door saying, "Honey, would you like to go to summer school with Mrs. Russell or go with us to Disneyland next week?" I never saw the wee girl again.

So I led short Bible studies at the breakfast table with the boys. The reaction? Sighs, eye-rolling and asking where they could find more to eat. At times, there seemed to be so little feedback, I thought I was talking to the napkins. In spite of that, I persisted.

My young men both left home, announcing they were glad to be out from under the rules of the roost!

Only months later, I got a package from Travis, who had finished Army boot camp. Inside was a devotional inscribed with these words penned by my son: "Merry Christmas, Mom. God gave the greatest gift of all, but I thought this book would help in using that gift....Though there is such a distance between us, we can look to the Lord and know we are united in Christ. Merry Christmas and God bless you now and forever."

The next year, Lance wrote me too. "Things are awesome since I rededicated my life. People get along with me better. I smile more. I went grocery shopping, and for the first time in two months, I wasn't in the *ten items or less line!*"

I found myself wiping my eyes with a rag and saw that it was one of the boy's tattered cross country tee shirts. I cried even more as I realized that God had continued the work in them.

Moms, parents, and grandparents everywhere, persist as you raise your children knowing God. Your job is to plant the seeds. Count on God for the rest!

How do you worship God as a family each day?

Further study: Acts 9:36-42

Day 5

God and the Dentist Know All

You know when I sit and when I rise; you perceive my thoughts from afar. You discern my going out and my lying down; you are familiar with all my ways.

Psalm 139:2-3

Going to the dentist every six months for teeth cleaning falls in the same category as getting stitches. It's not fun, but I have to do it. I always let out a sigh when the masked man finds no cavities.

I had pretended that I was taking good care of my teeth. Just before I went, I brushed, flossed, used the electric toothbrush and the little rubber pick. Just before all that sparkling hygiene, I had been licking the frosting center out of chocolate sandwich cookies. Yum! In my lunch every day was something sweet. Even though I limited the quantity and made everything from scratch, all were sweetened. Did I brush often? More days than I could count, I dropped into bed after work without brushing.

Would the dentist know?

As a reading teacher, I knew immediately when a child had not been practicing reading at home, no matter what the child or a parent said.

One day, I awoke with my jaw throbbing. When I brushed my teeth and wiggled painful teeth, I thought I had a loose crown. The dentist allowed me in as an emergency patient. After checking me over thoroughly, he said my teeth had become sensitive and recommended a dental rinse. Somewhere in the far reaches of my brain, I now faintly recalled, he had told me before to use the rinse every day. I did not. "What's making it hurt so bad?" I asked the dentist.

"Well, you have quite a bit of food particles caught in your teeth."

So there. He knew all along.

In our relationship with God, there is no room for pretending. He knows our hearts. Are you pretending or have you been sincere and honest with God?

Further study: Psalm 24:3-4

Day 6

All Things Orange and Healthy

Then he turned to his disciples and said privately, "Blessed are the eyes that see what you see."
Luke 10:23

At the grocery store, Maggie struggled as she rolled a bag of carrots onto her cart.

It was the size of a soldier's duffel bag! Thanksgiving was long past and its large family gatherings. Thinking she knew an irresistible health tip I did not, I asked, "What are you doing with all those carrots?"

Maggie smiled, "I juice them! You know what it's like working in the schools when the children come to school sick and sneeze across the table. I haven't been sick at all for six months! Not even a sniffle!"

Convinced of the great value of even more carrots, I hefted a fifty-pound bag of orange veggies in my cart. Whoops! The romaine lettuce and spinach in the bottom were as flat as a spatula.

After two hours of peeling and juicing, I had enough pulp and orange-colored peelings on the floor and counter to compost my tulip bed as well as all the bulb plantations in Holland. I'm embarrassed to tell you how little juice I got. The juice wasn't bad, but it wasn't apple juice, V-8, or chocolate milk.

When I heard a community member was very ill following chemo treatment, I zeroed in on a recipe that I like from a cookbook centered on healing with food. As I cooked up a gallon of carrot and cilantro soup, I knew it was just the ticket for boosting the immune system! When I called, her grandson said she was still getting chemo, but he would tell her. The next day, I left two more messages on the answering machine. No return calls.

Meanwhile, my refrigerator was dominated by all things carrot, and I still had fifteen pounds in a bag in the corner! When I heard of another very ill lady, I tried to pawn some soup off on her. No return calls, either. I called a friend for sympathy over the carrots. She said that the sick people want familiar comfort food, not healthy food. She added, "That's why they let patients in a hospital pick out anything they want to eat." By now, I couldn't look at anything in the eye that started as a carrot.

My generous supply of raw carrots, bagged in the corner of my kitchen, were beginning to smell a little earthy, like garden compost. Separating the bad ones into a bag for compost, I rescued the rest. This time, the healthy veggies became a sweet sauce with sugar, cinnamon, nutmeg, and fresh vanilla. That was more like it! The sauce had an exotic enticing flavor. Now the possibilities were endless! I could add a few ingredients and pass the carrots off as the award-winning resort recipe "Individual Sweet Potato Soufflé" or top it with a sweet nutty crunch mix and make the dessert my friends raved about. What about topping waffles with it as you would applesauce? Hallelujah! None of the carrots would go to waste!

Like the saga of my fifty pounds of carrots and the quest to turn it into healing foods, I have learned that we have endless ways of passing on the wonderful message of God in our hearts. It may be a matter of altering your recipe or putting your "before God and after" story into a form they can enjoy, like my sweet carrot sauce.

How has God changed your life for the better?

Further study: Colossians 3:12-14

Day 7

The Tarantula Tarantella

> *God made the wild animals according to their kinds, livestock according to their kinds, and all the creatures that move along the ground according to their kinds. And God saw that it was good.* Genesis 1:25

When the air conditioning is on full blast in a tent, it does not help much, especially in a remote area on the prickly desert floor. In tent terms, that meant all the screened picture windows, doors and skylight were unzipped to the moonlight. Dark outcroppings of bare rock still radiated the heat of the day on a spring night. My thighs were glued together with sweat. Late as it had been, I heard my sons softly breathing. While they were catching zzzzzs, I couldn't sleep. It was going to be a loooong night! I sat up and sighed.

Nearly as bright as sunup with a full moon, the land sparkled like mica. I peered through the screened window, appreciating the quiet sounds of a peaceful night. A very small breeze touched the desert creosote bushes and the mesquite trees.

As I listened and watched, I noticed a score of dark shapes each about the size of a fist crawl to center stage. Looking more closely, I saw the shapes had legs. They were giant tarantula spiders, tuning up like an orchestra before a performance. Then they began to dance in the moonlight like a troupe of professional folk dance performers! First, to the right, then to the left, spin around, strut and kick, dip and bow! Though I learned later dancing is normal spring courtship behavior for the male spiders, I think on the tarantulas doing the tarantella as a way to honor their Creator *and* their women!

Every day, we have to make a commitment to dedicate our minds, bodies and spirits to honor the Creator. Our actions truly reflect what is inside.

How have you made a commitment to honor God today?

Further study: Luke 19:28-40; Romans 12:1

Questions

The Wow Factor of You—Before and After!

Prayer partners give us another force for believing in the power of prayer. Sometimes, the smallest change can make a big difference. You can do this over the phone, calling a specific day and time every week. With my prayer partners, we planned a change after a very tough year. We added a celebration meal to share and review God's answered prayers. What difference did it make? We remembered our celebration all year with joyful hearts. We held God in awe at the way he handled our problems.

How do you worship?

What change can you make to improve your prayer life?

Reflections:

So live that you wouldn't be ashamed
to sell the family parrot to the town gossip.

Will Rogers

Week 15

Walk With Jesus as Your Model

Day 1

God is Taking Care of Me!

Let the peace of Christ rule in your hearts, since as members of one body you were called to peace.

Colossians 3:15

The older couple walked carefully through the parking lot on their way to their car, each a little bent at the shoulders. Victoria steadied herself with a cane while Jim walked ahead with the basket. They were smiling at the clear sunny winter day. They had been remembering the family reunion of children, grandchildren and great grandchildren just a few days earlier. It had been the culmination of love and their more than fifty years together.

Victoria felt a bump against her legs, fell, and cried, "My legs! My legs!" Jim turned to see she was down on freezing pavement with the front of a car over her. The multi-tasking driver had not seen the older woman. Neither had she heard the car. Quickly, someone called an ambulance. A crowd gathered and two men covered Victoria with their coats. While in the growing crowd of onlookers, most murmured about liability, lawyers, insurance and how terrible it was someone could so thoughtlessly run over an eighty-something year old woman, Victoria just lay quietly. The car's driver gasped, and then wound up with cries of panic, "Oh, I'm sorry! I'm so sorry!" Victoria gestured the woman to come next to her. Pulling her arm out from under the coat, Victoria pointed and wagged her finger at the young woman as she would have at any of her grown grandchildren. "Now, you stop that right now!" Victoria's voice was firm and authoritative, and the crowd hushed. "This was an accident! Accidents happen. Now, I'm going to be all right because **God is taking care of me!** You need to stop worrying and calm down."

When the request for prayer came over the prayer chain, it was for Victoria's injuries, but for the driver, too. Wouldn't you know it? Adding the driver to the prayer chain had been Victoria's doing.

Like Jesus when he walked the earth, Victoria modeled *selfless* living.

What can you do in your daily life that models Jesus' attitude?

Further study: Psalm 9:1-2

Day 2

A Legacy of Hospitality

> Jesus said, *"For I was hungry and you gave me something to eat. I was thirsty and you gave me something to drink, I was a stranger and you invited me in, I needed clothes and you clothed me, I was sick and you looked after me, I was in prison and you came to visit me."* Matthew 25:35

You could count on it. If the doorbell rang, my mother, Jeane, swung the door open with a smile and called out, "Come in! Are you hungry?"

Hospitality is truly a spiritual gift.

However, as a teen, I didn't always appreciate Mom's wildly enthusiastic invitations.

Most of the time on our family's modest income, we were sharing hot dogs (with or without bread), oatmeal, beans, soups with chopped franks, pancakes, or macaroni and cheese. Sometimes as she scraped the black coating off toast, my mother quipped, "It's still good. Just add butter!"

One evening, for the first time in about three years, Jeane fixed a rare main dish, a fancy crab salad. All five of us looked with appreciation and awe at the mound of crab on each of our colorful beds of mixed types of lettuce, shredded carrots, and green pepper. It looked like an entrée at a fancy resort.

My father had just finished with the "Amen!" when the doorbell rang.

I groaned.

Jeane answered, scanning the family of five at the front door.

I cringed, hoping and praying not to hear her usual invite. Black teenaged clouds formed in my mind. I was wishing the doorbell had been disconnected, the house was dead-bolted and the family wouldn't be there at the door. I longed to keep all of my crab, but there wasn't any more. It was all on our plates.

Of course, Mom welcomed them with, "Come in! Are you hungry?"

We'd known the family for years and they had come to say goodbye. Hard-working, honest people who were once prosperous, these two professionals and their three teen children faced many challenges lately. They were moving out of town.

Do you remember how Jesus fed 5,000 (not counting the women and children) with five loaves and two fish? That's what happened that night. As ten of us ate crab salad for dinner, we all had enough. Then Mom brought out a dessert. I saw the faces of our friends relax. They were grateful for our company and sharing this special crab dinner.

Mom truly understood the rest of what Jesus said in Matthew 25:40: *"The King will reply, 'I tell you the truth, whatever you did for one of least of these brothers of mine, you did for me.'*

I have learned from her and Jesus, now sharing time and meals with people.

When I hear the doorbell ring, can you guess how I answer?

"Come in! Are you hungry?"

How can you help others today? It could be as simple as a smile, a snack, or listening.

Further study: 2 Kings 4:42-44

Day 3

The Streetwalker of Snowflake

Teach me your way, O Lord, and I will walk in your truth; give me an undivided heart, that I may fear your name. Psalm 86:11

"I'm the streetwalker of Snowflake!" Sylvia told me the first time I caught up with her on her daily trek across the conservative community of Snowflake, Arizona.

As I rode alongside her on my bicycle—unable to keep up with her walking pace—I began to understand the kind of hooker she was.

Snow sprinkled over her red beret and matching all-weather coat. The middle-aged lady had tramped purposefully the full length of the town four days a week, a total of seven miles, and all other days three miles, for a total of more than forty miles every week!

Her own story had started as a 24/7 caretaker for her husband. "I had to clear the cobwebs out of my mind," she explained as she stepped out under the clear starry skies. While her husband slept, Sylvia had begun to walk. It had felt good. She had kept it up as a daily routine until arthritis had progressed, and Sylvia's knees throbbed with so much pain, she went to an orthopedic surgeon. The diagnosis was no cartilage left in her knees, the padding between the bones. Bone ground on bone with each step. The surgeon said, "Most people in your condition are in a wheelchair." But walking? He couldn't recommend it.

"What do I do about the pain?" she wanted to know.

"A total knee replacement," he offered. She refused, recognizing how much time and help she would need to recover.

She could not care for her husband with such serious surgery herself.

"What if I keep walking?" she wanted to know. The surgeon shrugged. "It can't get any worse. Go ahead if you want to." Sylvia enlisted reinforcements from her prayer group. They asked for a miracle! Sylvia's pain disappeared and she continued walking for another purpose.

"This is my mission that God has given me—to be a witness to the whole town!" Younger people became motivated to exercise and walk on a regular basis because of

Sylvia. Her walking partners—those that could keep up—were her captive audience for learning about God and the strength he gives.

She chuckled as she waved me off. "I'm back to work now as the streetwalker of Snowflake!" Sylvia tramped on her way in her daily service of the Lord.

What new way can your serve others in your daily life?

Further study: 1 Chronicles 29:11-13

Day 4

Raise Up Your Voice!

Then Jesus came to them and said, "All authority in heaven and on earth has been given to me. Therefore go and make disciples of all nations, baptizing them in the name of the Father and of the Son and of the Holy Spirit, and teaching them to obey everything I have commanded you." Matthew 28:18-20

With a wide Western hat in hand dotted with round drops of rain, Dave stomped the mud off his boots as he and his wife came inside for the Cowboy Church services. Around Dave's neck was a faded blue bandana. He smiled at the friends around the room he visited often and found a seat next to a family he knew well. Rob patted the older gentlemen on the shoulder, and his two children ran into Dave's arms for a hug.

Close to the end of the service, Pastor Steve asked for prayer requests and wrote those down. "Let's hear it for the 'praises' this week! What are the by golly, great things God has done in your lives?" After many shared, Dave stood and pulled his bandana down just a bit.

"Montrose, Colorado, is the most beautiful country I've ever seen," he began telling about a recent trip there to the high country carpeted with grass, wildflowers and tall trees. "We all got together around a big campfire outside," he said, "so much family was seated all around. I just filled up with joy! It was real nice. I told them about God in my life. But the most important thing about the whole trip," Dave paused, "was when my mother-in-law and grandsons decided to accept Jesus right there under the stars. I'll always remember it."

Dave had halted throughout his speech. He stopped to adjust the electronic device held to the tracheotomy at his throat. If Dave can do that with less sound and volume than most of us have, what can we do with our voices?

Further study: Galatians 3:26-29

Day 5

Let Your Light Shine!

You are the light of the world. A city on a hill cannot be hidden. Matthew 5:14

Bridegroom Travis and his new wife, Maria, leaving their wedding in formal attire, had just boarded a small boat that shuttled them to their honeymoon in a lighthouse. We waved them off, spotting the white lighthouse with red trim across the water in the distance. The next afternoon, the newlyweds excitedly called shore, "You have to see this place! It's incredible!" By phone, they arranged for a friend to shuttle wedding guests to the island for an impromptu dinner.

Ring-bearer, five-year-old Eric, ran up and down the stairs, explored every room of the vacation villa, as well as the tiny lounge where a light had once been. He breathlessly commented, "This is a good home for retirement!"

Travis peered at the kindergarten boy. Where had he been learning about retirement, I.R.A.s, stocks, and investments?

"Retirement?" Travis asked.

"Yes," explained Eric. "That's when you *break up* with your job."

Do we ever retire from doing things for others to honor God, thanking and worshiping him? Never. Like the lighthouse that once kept ships safe in dangerous water, we are a light to others in our everyday life. Lighthouses have been replaced by satellites, but God's lights never stop shining.

How much of the Jesus' walk do others see in us?

Further study: Isaiah 60:19

Day 6

Who Burned Their Lunch?

> *As Jesus and his disciples were on their way, he came to a village where a woman named Martha opened her home to him. She had a sister called Mary, who sat at the Lord's feet listening to what he said.*
>
> Luke 10:38-39

Bill, a young father, was in the lounge when I threw my knee pads in the microwave to heat, slapped the control panel without looking and sat across from him to give him my full attention. I listened.

Bill's hat had been pulled down around his eyes to hide the redness and the streaks of tears as he had rushed into work that morning. Things had been more difficult than ever with his small children and marital struggles. While he had been working through family issues over the last few months, I had been nursing a serious knee injury that I had worried was worse because of walking nearly eight hours on my shift. Every break, I heated my knee pads, sat down with a sigh and slapped them on each knee like dumplings.

Soon black smoke boiled out of the microwave! More smoke coughed out when I opened the door and fanned it. Now the knee pads, stuffed with cracked corn that popped, were as thick as a family-sized stack of hamburger patties.

Rick came in first with his vest pulled over his nose, "Who burned the popcorn?"

His department wasn't far away. But soon Randy came coughing into the lounge from the far west in the store, "Geez! Whose lunch caught fire?" Then there was Michelle from the far east where live birds and the lovely fragrance of flowers normally smelled better than any part of the huge store. "Where's the fire?

What happened?" When the growing crowd from the east, west, north and south checked the lounge to see if the fire department needed to extinguish a blaze, I told Michelle I was responsible for the disaster. She commented, "***You, Jo***? I can't believe it! Don't you take *gourmet cooking lessons*?"

After cleaning the microwave, emptying the trash, and tossing the wet and smoking black knee pads in the dumpster outside, I remembered I had done the right thing giving my full attention to Bill. My first priority had been to listen when it was needed the most. Listening had been the Master's work, just as with Mary.

Who may need time today to talk while you listen?

Further study: Luke 10:40-42

Day 7

Walk in Jesus' Steps

And whatever you do, whether in word or deed, do it all in the name of the Lord Jesus, giving thanks to God the Father through him. Colossians 3:17

"You can give me any female roommate you want as long as she doesn't drink, smoke, or snore," I commented in my call to the organizers of an out-of-state conference center. I needed housing for a Christian writers' conference.

Though I'd been to dozens of teaching conferences, I was attending my first writers' conference ever. Anxious to make a good impression, I thought long and hard about the necessities for traveling and staying four days in the mountain conference center.

Determined I wouldn't show up looking like a country woman, I narrowed priorities down. (After all, one bellman at a fancy metro hotel will always remember helping me haul home-grown pumpkins to my twenty-third floor room in a mirrored glass elevator. The pumpkins had been a gift for a friend in the city.) Produce was out for this trip!

Just a few days before I left, I found out that unlike teacher conferences where you exchanged addresses on paper napkins or whatever free notepads were in the registration packet, I needed business cards. A friend's computer coughed out a dozen colored cards, and then died. Jesus had twelve disciples who were able to do the job, and I had twelve business cards. They would have to do.

Peggy, my roomie, had settled in and organized everything on her side by color and category. Her clothes were as neat as new fashions in a designer salon.

Four trips up two flights of stairs with a bicycle on my shoulder, boxes of juice, groceries, clothes, and a blender, and I'd done my aerobic exercise for the day. Peggy had a teeny smile as she watched me unpack. Then she asked,

"You want to go to the cafeteria for dinner?"

"I wasn't planning to. I brought food," I told her.

"Are you going for breakfast there tomorrow?" she wanted to know.

"Nope. I've got granola and fruit shakes."

"Okay, I'll see you in a little bit, then," she said.

When Peggy returned, she handed me an envelope. "This is for you."

"What is it?"

"It's a meal ticket. You need to be in the cafeteria to sit with the editors, publishers and writers. I've been to five of these conferences, so I know."

Tears moistened my eyes. Even without my bringing pumpkins, Peggy had sized up my naïve preparation for the conference. It didn't include a meal ticket.

"Why would you do this?" I asked, still stunned. "We only just met."

"Because *I can*," Peggy explained.

We are Jesus' hands on this earth. He still walks and is alive in us. Peggy walked as Jesus did. It showed in her actions.

What can you do to help someone today?

Further study: Galatians 5:22-23

Questions

Walk With Jesus as Your Model

One pastor suggested that when he goes to a restaurant, he tells the waitress, "We are just about ready to ask for a blessing on this food. Is there anything you would like us to pray for as well?" He follows this with asking, "Do you want us to pray for you now or later?"

Another told how one question can open a door wherever you are. He ends any transaction at the store or restaurant with, "May God bless you today!"

Determine what your spiritual gifts are and write them here. For internet help, you can target a guide with a search for "spiritual gifts test."

In what areas of your life can you walk more like Jesus today?

Reflections:

Conclusion

Now that you've walked this spiritual road, you know the facts of life! God loves you! You are gifted! You are chosen! You are special! God isn't finished with your life and journey yet!

Each of you has a different circle of influence shining with your light of love. There is no one else who has your same influence! The whole world is where you use your gifts: at home, in the work world, balancing many duties, pulling yourself up by the bootstraps, going to school, raising children, running committees or your own business, generating winning ideas or enjoying retirement. Christ is with you to work. If you have got your hands full, know that God gives you another one—his!

Do you know your gifts? What do you love to do well? That's a start. Listening, cooking, writing out cards, serving a meal, babysitting, encouraging, fixing things and helping out are some avenues for using gifts. If you are still doubtful, you can search under "spiritual gifts test." On Google, it brings over 550,000 hits.

Close to the time widowed Eleanor joyfully walked down the aisle again, she said, "Here's the teacher's guide. You can take over the class." It was for the "Faithful Friends" class with members from nineteen to ninety-two years old. Just as the shepherds who heard the great news of Jesus' birth, I was afraid! All day long, I had little people who often clung to my leg. During a science activity in which we had pasted up parts of the human body, one wailed, "Mrs. Russell! Someone took my bladder!" The women's class was entirely different, with many hurting from the loss of spouses and family. Yet, we have grown together.

Others also share their gifts. Jane leads and teaches people to make quilts, bouquets and silk corsages for the local nursing homes. She creates small decorated canvas bags filled with materials to welcome the newcomers to a small church. At last count, she had given out over 500 of these welcome bags in two years.

Dee adds to her job responsibilities at a large retail store by identifying, tagging and distributing building materials donated to non-profit organizations.

Sharon, an office manager, became a Chamber of Commerce member and sets a Christian example by modeling God's values in each of the community decisions brought to the Chamber.

JoAnn, widowed in mid-life, runs her late husband's hardware store, modeling Christ's values in all the training and time she invests in training her employees.

Imogene and Don dedicated every Monday afternoon and evening after work to spend with eighty-something-year-old Stella. The elderly lady, who had no family left, had cared for Imogene and Don's children decades before when they were young.

Walk into Linda's house anytime and you see the Bible open on the table and smell wonderful food. She is a retired owner of a roadhouse café and trucking business that started "The Basket and Bag Ladies" community outreach program, visiting those who need encouragement.

Every one of us is born with diamond dust inside. It's God's gift. Some are already diamonds, honed into a gem because of challenges, heartbreak, and loss. Some are diamonds in the rough. God is still shaping you.

Let who you are sparkle as you get brighter and more valuable. How will you serve him with your gifts?

Three things are needed for success:
a backbone, a wishbone, and a funny bone.

The Funny Bone Connection

Between God and Woman

Doctors have been thrilled to learn fairly recently that laughter and humor help put things in perspective, serve as good stress relief, promote healing, and aid in our coping with the challenges of life.

I imagine God chuckled at man's revelation of the value of humor, "I knew it would take them a long time to catch on, but I invented the jokes, humor, laughter, grins, and chortling. Those that seek them will find them all through the Bible! I made people in my own image, and each one includes a funny bone, too!"

Here is a modernized journey through some of the Bible's humor. It is fictionalized. Read the real thing in the Bible.

ADAM AND EVE

The setting was the lush outdoor room and patio at Adam and Eve's. They stood by a fruit tree. Each munched on a piece of fresh fruit.

"Adam, where are you hiding?" God asked, and a nearby serpent high-tailed it behind a fountain.

Adam answered, "We haven't got a thing to wear, not even Fruit of the Looms! Eve added, "So we need to get to the mall this morning and go shopping. "Could you please give us a credit card?"

"Who told you about being naked, the mall, and a credit card? Have you eaten from the fruit of this tree I said was off-limits?"

"Well, the serpent made us do it….Where did he go?" Adam asked as he looked around for the beautiful creature. He saw the tip of Sam Serpent's tail and pointed.

God then asked the woman, "What have you done?"

"Sorry, God! Adam is tired of my salads. I thought the serpent was giving me a new recipe!"

JONAH

Jonah is famous for procrastination when he had an unpleasant job to do. God told him to take three days and walk the streets of Nineveh telling the people God had seen their wickedness and would destroy them and the whole city, including the best tourist attraction—a family water park!

Instead, Jonah watched minutes tick by as he sat at his computer, checking his e-mail. Right there in black and white was "Last Minute Cheap Cruise Vacations to Your Dream Destination!" He clicked. Sure enough, they went anywhere in the world except Nineveh. He clicked on the "Learn more" to find one "Rustic cargo ship makes four to twenty day trips across the Mediterranean. Our specialty includes sea food cuisine prepared by an award-winning chef. You can join the crew for the hands-on experience of a lifetime, deep water fishing. Equipment is provided! Many land excursions available."

Jonah needed a vacation. Being a prophet was hard work twenty-four seven. Why, the phone rang at all hours, clients texted him on his cell phone, and his mission territory was huge. He clicked on the "purchase now," packed his duffle, fishing hat, and as soon as his payment was confirmed, left the computer and phones at home. Jonah decided God would have to wait. He was already visualizing a trophy catch. That didn't happen. Instead, the cruise crew lightened the load during a storm and threw Jonah overboard. Jonah opened his eyes to an entirely different venue and a distinct new smell. Instead of a dinner of Supreme Fish Almondine with fresh steamed spinach and baked, stuffed figs, he looked around at a wet, dark, breathing, belching wall of flesh surrounded by all things dead from bits and pieces of the large fish's breakfast. Jonah's dinner was on hold. So was breakfast, lunch, and dinner the next day, and the next. After three days and nights with no cuisine at all, Jonah told God he would follow directions. God had the fish spit him out on dry land, conveniently located close to the train station that took him to Nineveh.

WHEN JESUS SAID, "DON'T TELL ANYONE!"

When Jesus walked the earth, his miracles were legendary. Jesus cured many illnesses. How many times did he tell them not to tell?

In Matthew 8, the Bible tells of a man who left his dermatologist with bad news. His condition was hopeless, no cure. Then he saw a crowd hurrying along and wanted to find out where and why they were hustling, so he tagged along. Part of his ears were gone. His fingers were white powdery stubs. The others saw his skin and backed away. But Jesus was there, ready to help and to touch.

The man caught up with him and kneeled, "Lord, if you are willing, you can make me clean." All it took was Jesus' light touch. Fingers and ears that disappeared five years before—now he wiggled them! His skin was smooth and clear! Then Jesus said, "See that you don't tell anyone!" (Matt. 8:3) Jesus added that he needed to go to the priest and make an offering. But the top secret part was more difficult. As he was leaping and jumping around on feet that didn't hurt anymore, wiggling fingers and ears, waving down folks who were passing by, he yelled, "Hey, folks! I'm a whole man! Look at me! Just look!"

Does that sound like a secret to you? So much for classified information!

WILL THE MOST UNLIKELY CANDIDATES PLEASE STEP FORWARD?

God picks unlikely applicants. Many times, they did not even apply.

RAHAB

What about Rahab, in Joshua 2:4, known for her success in the oldest profession in the world? She was Jesus' ancestor. Rahab had a successful establishment in the city wall area, with not one, but five picture windows facing the cobblestone street, and a shapely girl in each one. Today, she herself was a well-dressed business woman, bulging out in sexy curves in a corset push-up top and thong. Her dark curly hair hung to her shoulders. Two foreigners came by. Their money was as green as anyone else's. She smiled, nodded, and gestured with her fingers for them to come inside for the time of their lives! But they weren't interested in her or her girls' usual services. They wanted a place to hide, as they were spies. By reputation, she knew their armies, their powerful God and their victories! Rahab had good reason to be afraid. She made a trade: their lives for hers and that of her family.

Rahab retired her thong, jewelry, and "miracle" push up bra for a Mrs. Degree.

She married an Israelite, one of the invaders. Check out Matthew 1 for Rahab's full family line.

GIVE GOD YOUR IMPOSSIBLE DREAMS!

Abram and his childless wife Sarai lived in an assisted living facility, enjoying all of the amenities—a walk-in tub, the pool, cards, bingo, and two meals a day that neither of them had to cook.

The sign at the entrance to Heavenly Valley Resort read, "A friendly gated community for seniors catering to all your needs. NO CHILDREN ALLOWED."

"Fat chance of that," thought ninety-nine-year-old Abram as he sighed and lowered himself into the soothing waters of the hot tub. Some time earlier, God had promised Abram a son of his own, an heir of his own body and Sarai's. So far, any attempts in that area had backfired.

Shortly afterwards, God showed up with a new message. Now Abram was to call himself Abraham and his wife, Sarai, by the name Sarah. They were getting kicked out of the Heavenly Valley Resort in nine months! The reason? Abraham rolled on the deck with laughter, "Will a son be born to a man a hundred years old? Will Sarah bear a child at the age of ninety?" (Gen. 17:17)

He thought to himself, "Sarah's gone through change of life. You can't fool Mother Nature!"

God, reading his thoughts, reminded him, "I AM MOTHER NATURE!"

Reaffirming his promise that Abraham would have descendents as numerous as sand on a beach, or M and M's during holidays, God gave the happy couple an only son, Isaac. The young man did his duty in the descendents department. God kept his word!

God gets our attention with humor, and gives it to us a moment at a time as we need it. Why? Because no matter how challenging our burdens are, God knows we will laugh and make it through!

About the Author

Jo Russell

Writer, columnist, Sunday school teacher, and speaker Jo Russell keeps us laughing at every day challenges through her experiences as a single mom raising sons from diapers to adulthood. Jo reaches out to show others how to help themselves and to believe that with God, all things are possible.

Jo is a retired reading teacher, who pursued a career in retail sales, learning much about the how-to and fix-it business. These skills are often needed by women who are trying to fix a toilet while the doorbell is ringing and one of the children smashes another's finger in the door.

She has won several national writing contests for humor, including the Society of Southwestern Authors humor award. Her inspirational stories, devotionals, and humor have been in dozens of magazines including *Open Windows* and *Arizona Highways.* She is a contributing author in *Chicken Soup for the Soul—Shaping the New You* (December, 2010), and *Heavenly Humor for the Dieter's Soul* (October, 2011.)

Jo lives in a small northeast Arizona town and loves it. You can contact her at jorussell3@yahoo.com.

Selected Bibliography

Barnes, Emilie. Author and speaker, Glorietta Christian Writers' Conference, Glorietta, New Mexico, October, 2004. [Week 9 questions]

God-inspired authors et al. *Life Application Study Bible: New International Version,* Tyndale House Publishers, Inc., Illinois, and Zondervan Publishing House, Michigan, 1997.

Fairchild, Mary, "Christianity—4 Essentials to Spiritual Growth." http://christianity.about.com/od/practicaltools/a/spiritualgrowth.htm. Accessed February 13, 2011. [Week 13 questions]

Delsasso, Sylvia, Snowflake, Arizona. Interview October, 2005. [The Streetwalker of Snowflake]

Exploring the Southwest Desert USA, "Common Questions About Tarantulas." http://www.desertusa.com/july96/du_taran.html. Accessed January 24, 2011. [The Tarantula Tarantella]

Impact Factory Homepage, "Public Speaking." http://www.impactfactory.com/p/category_public_speaking_skills_training_development.h. Accessed January 16, 2011. [In My Heart, There Is A Melody]

Kurtus, Ron, "Winston Churchill's 'Never Give In' Speech of 1941." May 8, 2010. http://www.school-for-champions.com./speeches/churchill_never_give_in.htm. Accessed February 2, 1011. [Let's Hear it for Bionic Women]

Phillips, Bob. *Phillips' Treasury of Humorous Quotations,* Tyndale House Publishers, Inc., Illinois, 2004.

Rose Publishing, "Names of God from the Old Testament." Rose Bible e-chart, http://www.rose-publishing.com. [God by Any Other Name is Good]

Teugels, GG. and D.F.E. Thys van den Audenaerde, Fishbase.org. "Tilapia zillii—Redbelly tilapia" http://www.fishbase.org/Summary/SpeciesSummary.php?id=1390. Accessed January 4, 2011. [Seth's Secret for Making Work More Fun]

Twist, Steve, "Remembering victims key to death penalty—Executing justice: Arizona's moral dilemma." May 20, 2007. http://www.azcentral.com/arizonarepublic/viewpoints/articles/0520twist-520.html. Accessed January 13, 2011. [Danger in the Wilderness]

Do you need a speaker?

Do you want Jo Russell to speak to your group or event? Then contact Larry Davis at: (623) 337-8710 or email: ldavis@intermediapr.com or use the contact form at: www.intermediapr.com.

Whether you want to purchase bulk copies of *Which Button Do You Push to Get God to Come Out?* or buy another book for a friend, get it now at: www.imprbooks.com.

If you have a book that you would like to publish, contact Terry Whalin, Publisher, at Intermedia Publishing Group, (623) 337-8710 or email: twhalin@intermediapub.com or use the contact form at: www.intermediapub.com.